THE
REASON
WHY

THE
REASON
WHY

An Anthology of the Murderous Mind

Edited, with an Introduction by

RUTH RENDELL

Crown Publishers, Inc.
New York

Published by Crown Publishers, Inc., 201 East 50th Street, New York, New York 10022. Member of the Crown Publishing Group.

Random House, Inc. New York, Toronto, London, Sydney, Auckland

Originally published in the Great Britain by Jonathan Cape, Ltd., in 1995.

CROWN is a trademark of Crown Publishers, Inc.

Manufactured in the United States of America

Library of Congress Cataloging-in-Publication Data (tk)
The reason why: an anthology of the murderous mind / edited with an
    introduction by Ruth Rendell. —1st ed.
    1. Death—Literary collections.   2. Murder—Psychological aspects.
3. Detective and mystery stories.   I. Rendell, Ruth
PN6071.D4R43   1996
808.8'0355—dc20   95-52622

ISBN 0-517-70347-5

10 9 8 7 6 5 4 3 2 1

First American Edition

CONTENTS

INTRODUCTION

Murder itself is not interesting. It is the impetus to murder, the passions and terrors which bring it to pass and the varieties of feeling surrounding the act that make of a sordid or revolting event compulsive fascination. Even the most ardent readers of detective fiction are not much preoccupied with whether a Colt Magnum revolver or a Bowie knife was used to despatch the victim. The perpetrator's purpose, the 'why', is what impels them to read on. They need to find out what has gone on in his head, whether revealed through action, dialogue, mental activity or the stream of consciousness. They need to follow what goes on in the minds of those others who come within his range, observe him, fear him or suffer at his hands.

In compiling this anthology, I tried to keep this always in mind. I was not cataloguing murders. I was not collecting examples of stabbings and shootings, stranglings and what Wilde calls 'strange manners of poisoning'. This book was not to be a collection of murder samples from the vast number of true crime works—the majority of them gratuitously ghoulish and indifferently written—nor of acts conceived by crime novelists, however good, however secure their place in literature. My extracts were to be all in the mind, all in the talk, the imagination, the dreams, the boastings and the remorse of people who had killed in fact and in fiction; from their thoughts and from those of observers and bystanders who wondered at their acts and commented on what they had done. Motive, not action; speculation and opinion; thought and theory, not performance.

It is no more necessary, of course, to have committed murder in order to write about it than it is for the writer of sea stories to have been in the navy or a chronicler of the sixteenth century to have been born in the reign of Elizabeth I. In fact, whereas these latter must have studied their subject and put in long hours of research, the novelist, playwright or poet who employs murder needs only the writer's imagination and an understanding of the darker side of the human soul. If we have not all wanted at some time or another to commit murder, we have all considered what it must be like so to want. We have all said, 'I could kill him!' and meant it—for a few moments. Such thoughts in a good or a great writer have led to that understanding mentioned earlier, to a putting down on paper motivations and impulses at least as true as those of 'real' murderers, and to an elucidation of the murderous mind impossible to the inarticulate and the inhibited.

For that reason I have used in this anthology far more extracts from literature and good crime fiction than from accounts of actual homicides, though these of course have their place. I have assumed that if some great writer of the past or present tells us that a man or woman intends to commit murder for such and such a reason, feels this or that about it or looks back on it with this or that particular emotion, then these examinations and conclusions are valid. If Sophocles tells us that certain sensations of doom and destiny passed through the mind of Oedipus after he had killed his father, and Shakespeare that specific kinds of fear and indecision afflicted Macbeth before the murder of Duncan, I have taken these to be at least as true as the feelings of an actual assassin.

Extracts from these writers will be found here. Among the Greek dramatists and Shakespeare's contemporaries and successors, it was not a matter of finding apt passages but of choosing a few among the many. To these playwrights death by violence was the stuff of life and it would not be putting it too strongly to say that tragedy for an Elizabethan or Jacobean either meant the why and how of murder or somehow involved it. Interestingly, here too, motive was of some importance, but the murderer's mind far more so. In spite of the play within the play and the ingenious murder method, we do not much care how Claudius killed Hamlet's father, nor why, for this is obvious, but we are to this day still fascinated by his thoughts, his fears and his prayers.

Gain, jealousy and fear are said to be the three reasons for murder, but as I began my research I found many more. I found subdivisions of those three as well as strange, hitherto unconsidered motivations.

Altruism is not generally thought of in this connection but I came across instances of killing for rescue or salvation, death meted out to save someone from a fate seen as worse than death, and these cases so moving that I hesitated before including them. Is murder, after all, still murder when the motive is mercy?

For good or ill, I kept them and they are to be found here, as are those who committed murder 'because it seemed right', as Hardy's Tess did. Others did so from a sense of duty, from madness and, strangest of all, for the sake of murder. Literature, like life, has murderers who killed to see what it was like, just to have done it, simply to understand a sensation few of us, fortunately, will ever know.

There is a difference between those internally spoken words 'I could kill him!' and the positive contemplation of murder. The former quickly passes, is perhaps never seriously meant, but the latter is a brooding obsessive thing that can take over the personality and corrupt the mind; all that is lacking between intent and act may only be opportunity or the reaching out of a hand. No one exemplified this better than George Eliot when in *Daniel Deronda* she wrote of Gwendolen Harleth's passionate desire to see her husband dead at the moment of his accidental death by drowning. And what of Arnold Bennett's flighty young matron who pauses not an instant before saying the words that will murder the mandarin and secure her fourteen shillings and fivepence?

Motives for murder have been diverse and strange both in reality and in the literary imagination. Could any account be more bizarre than Rachel de Queiroz's story of the man who killed the postman because it was he who brought his wife letters from her lover? Only perhaps in life when Major Armstrong made up twenty little packets of arsenic allegedly for the individual poisoning of dandelions. Could any be more chilling than Chappie in the Stanley Ellin story who kills an unknown man in order to extract from another an admission of inferiority? Or sadder than Tolstoy's tale of Aksenov who refuses to commit his fellow convict to a flogging even though the man is responsible for his imprisonment.

I have begun with those murdered within the family, for it is here that any investigating officer will first look for a perpetrator: parents and children, brothers, husbands and wives, lovers. They are followed by the killers seeking revenge, the vindication of honour and to avenge attacks on a woman's good name. Yet by far the most common motive for murder, it seemed to me when I was compiling this collection, was that of escape: escape from discovery, from an undesired marriage or other relationship, from debt, from shame and humiliation, from personal destruction, even from one's own psyche, and of course from retribution; Hardy's expert sempstress using her skills to avoid the attentions of a drunken husband; P. D. James's Mary Ducton who kills a child in a vain attempt to prevent her husband's sexual abuse coming to light; Gibbon's slaves who kill the Emperor before he can kill them.

Murder seems, in literature at any rate, inseparable from remorse, and fiction dwells so much on guilt and self-reproach, that for this section much more was rejected than selected. Poe's ever-beating heart haunting a murderer was an essential inclusion; so was Hood's poor usher, dogged by the 'horrid thing' that pursued his soul, and perhaps no one described more tellingly the consequences of consuming remorse and its ultimate redeeming effect than William Godwin in his account of the man who hunted and was hunted by Caleb Williams.

Psychopaths and serial killers are fashionable protagonists in fiction. In true crime writing and biography there is no lack of in-depth examinations of their mental processes. Some of the best of these are here but interspersed with extracts from the literature of the psychotic murderer, the writing of Graham Greene and, essentially, Norman Mailer.

Finally, I come to the irrational murders, the taking of another's life for no reason even remotely acceptable to the ordinary person. In some cases there seemed to be no motive at all, in others the unfortunate victim was a substitute or stand-in for a real or imagined offender. One man went out to find his father against whom he had cause for resentment; his victim was a passer-by whose tone of voice affronted him. A pair of amoral undergraduates killed a companion for the experience of committing the act. Camus's Outsider is here and

Truman Capote's killers of the Clutter family. Their victims were the ones who had to pay for the pain and rage induced by another and by another's acts.

This collection makes grim reading and, necessarily, light relief comes sparingly. But if these excerpts are chilling and contain their own despair, they are also enlightening. To some extent they answer the often-repeated question, 'How could they do it?' They deny the seemingly unarguable: 'It is all beyond belief!'

In them lies the dark side of human nature that is in us all, even the most innocent and blameless, and this they may reveal. They may serve as analysts to show what lies beneath the surface of our own controlled and purified consciousness. As much as anything, they teach understanding; not forgiveness, still less condonation, but an inkling that explanation may be possible. They teach some comprehension of the temptations, the desires, the anger or the fear that lead men and women to put an end to the life of a fellow human being. Mme de Stael was wrong when she said that to understand all is to forgive all: to understand is to understand, and that in itself is an immense step forward in human tolerance and human civilisation.

1

'O, HIDEOUS SEQUEL!'

In the Family

Most murders, we are told, are committed within the family. For if this is where love is, here also is hatred, resentment, the desire for revenge and escape. Husbands kill wives, wives husbands, parents their children and children their parents.

Oedipus was the first and most famous of all parricides. When he understands that he has killed his father and married his mother he inflicts upon himself a terrible punishment.

As if led on,
He smashes hollering through the double doors
breaking all its bolts and lunges in.
And there we saw her hanging, twisted, tangled,
from a halter—sight that wrings from him
a maddening cry. He frees the noose and lays
the wretched woman down, the—O
hideous sequel!—rips from off her dress
the golden brooches she was wearing, holds
them up and rams them home right through his eyes.
'Wicked, wicked eyes,' he gasps,
'You shall not see me nor my shame—
not see my present crime.
Go dark, for all time blind
to what you never should have seen, and blind
to those this heart has cried to see.'

And as this dirge went up so did his hands
to strike the founts of sight, not once but many times.
And all the while his eyeballs gushed
in bloody dew upon his beard ... no, not dew,
no oozing drops—a spurt
of black ensanguined rain like hail beat down.

A coupled punishment upon a coupled sin:
husband and wife one flesh in their disaster;
their happiness of long ago—true happiness—
now turned to tears this day; to ruin, death and shame;
no evil absent by whatever cursed name.

From *Oedipus the King* by Sophocles, fifth century BC,

translated from the Greek by Paul Roche

Cain was the first man to kill his brother.

Abel was a keeper of sheep but Cain was a tiller of the ground.

And in the process of time it came to pass, that Cain brought of the fruit of the ground an offering unto the Lord.

And Abel, he also brought of the firstlings of his flock and of the fat thereof. And the Lord had respect unto Abel and unto his offering:

But unto Cain and to his offering he had not respect. And Cain was very wroth, and his countenance fell.

And the Lord said unto Cain, Why art thou wroth? and why is thy countenance fallen?

If thou doest well, shalt thou not be accepted? and if thou doest not well, sin lieth at the door. And unto thee shall be his desire, and thou shalt rule over him.

And Cain talked with Abel his brother: and it came to pass, when they were in the field, that Cain rose up against Abel his brother, and slew him.

From *Genesis* IV

*Cain refuses to honour a god who desires blood sacrifice. In Byron's
drama he kills his brother to prevent more cruelty.*

ABEL (*kneeling*): Oh, brother, pray! Jehovah's wroth with thee.
CAIN: Why so?
ABEL:　　　　　Thy fruits are scattered on the earth.
CAIN: From earth they came, to earth let them return;
　　　Their seed will bear fresh fruit there ere the summer;
　　　Thy burst flesh-off'ring propers better; see
　　　How heaven licks up the flames, when thick with blood!
ABEL: Think not upon my offering's acceptance,
　　　But make another of thine own before
　　　It is too late.
CAIN:　　　　　I will build no more altars,
　　　Nor suffer any—
ABEL (*rising*):　Cain! What meanest thou?
CAIN: To cast down yon vile flatt'rer of the clouds,
　　　The smoky harbinger of thy dull prayers—
　　　Thine altar, with its blood of lambs and kids,
　　　Which fed on milk, to be destroyed in blood.
ABEL (*opposing him*): Thou shalt not:—add not impious works to
　　　impious
　　　Words! Let that altar stand—'tis hallowed now
　　　By the immortal pleasure of Jehovah,
　　　In his acceptance of the victims.
CAIN:　　　　　　　　　　　　　　*His!*
　　　His pleasure! What was his high pleasure in
　　　The fumes of scorching flesh and smoking blood,
　　　To the pain of the bleating mothers, which
　　　Still yearn for their dead offspring? Or the pangs
　　　Of the sad innocent victim underneath
　　　Thy pious knife? Give way! This bloody record
　　　Shall not stand in the sun, to shame creation!
ABEL: Brother, give back! Thou shalt not touch my altar
　　　With violence: if that thou wilt adopt it,

[5]

To try another sacrifice, 'tis thine.

CAIN: Another sacrifice! Give way, or else
That sacrifice may be—

ABEL: What meanst thou?

CAIN: Give—
Give way!—thy God loves blood!—then look to it:—
Give way, ere he hath *more*!

From *Cain* by Lord Byron, 1821

Beatrice Cenci was executed in 1599 for the murder of her cruel and tyrannical father. Her brother and stepmother suffered the same fate. The Cenci's final outrage on his daughter was rape, which is what Shelley refers to here.

LUCRETIA: Alas! What has befallen thee, child?
What has thy father done?

BEATRICE: What have I done?
Am I not innocent? Is it my crime
That one with white hair, and imperious brow,
Who tortured me from my forgotten years,
As parents only dare, should call himself
My father, yet should be!—Oh, what am I?
What name, what place, what memory shall be mine?
What retrospects, outliving even despair?

LUCRETIA: He is a violent tyrant, surely, child:
We know that death alone can make us free;
His death or ours. But what can he have done
Of deadlier outrage or worse injury?
Thou art unlike thyself; thine eyes shoot forth
A wandering and strange spirit. Speak to me,
Unlock those pallid hands whose fingers twine
With one another.

[6]

BEATRICE: 'Tis the restless life
     Tortured within them. If I try to speak
     I shall go mad. Ay, something must be done;
     What, yet I know not—something which shall make
     The thing that I have suffered but a shadow
     In the dread lightning which avenges it;
     Brief, rapid, irreversible, destroying
     The consequences of what it cannot cure.
     Some such thing is to be endured or done:
     When I know what, I shall be still and calm,
     And never anything will move me more.
     But now!—O blood, which art my father's blood,
     Circling through these contaminated veins,
     If thou, poured forth on the unpolluted earth,
     Could wash away the crime, and punishment
     By which I suffer—no, that cannot be!
     Many might doubt there was a God above
     Who sees, and permits evil, and so die:
     That faith no agony shall obscure in me.
LUCRETIA: It must indeed have been some bitter wrong;
     Yet what, I dare not guess. Oh, my lost child,
     Hide not in proud impenetrable grief
     Thy sufferings from my fear.
BEATRICE: I hide them not.
     What are the words which you would have me speak?
     I, who can feign no image in my mind
     Of that which has transformed me: I, whose thought
     Is like a ghost shrouded and folded up
     In its own formless horror: Of all words,
     That minister to mortal intercourse,
     Which wouldst thou hear? For there is none to tell
     My misery: if another ever knew
     Aught like to it, she died as I will die,
     And left it, as I must, without a name.

[7]

Death! Death! Our law and our religion call thee
A punishment and a reward...Oh, which
Have I deserved?
LUCRETIA: The peace of innocence;
Till in your season you be called to heaven.
Whate'er you may have suffered, you have done
No evil. Death must be the punishment
Of crime, or the reward of trampling down
The thorns which God has strewed upon the path
Which leads to immortality.
BEATRICE: Ay, death—
The punishment of crime. I pray thee, God,
Let me not be bewildered while I judge.
If I must live day after day, and keep
These limbs, the unworthy temple of thy spirit,
As a foul den from which what thou abhorrest
Make mock thee, unavenged—it shall not be!

From The Cenci *by Percy Bysshe Shelley, 1819*

Seduced and abandoned, Hetty has given birth to a child and, half-mad with fear and privation, dare not be encumbered by her baby. Dinah listens with compassion to her pathetic confession.

Hetty shuddered. She was silent for some moments, and when she began again, it was in a whisper.

'I came to a place where there was lots of chips and turf, and I sat down on the trunk of a tree to think what I should do. And all of a sudden I saw a hole under the nut-tree, like a little grave. And it darted into me like lightning—I'd lay the baby there, and cover it with the grass and the chips. I couldn't kill it any other way. And I'd done it in a minute; and, oh, it cried so, Dinah, I *couldn't* cover it quite up—I thought perhaps somebody 'ud come and take care of it, and then it wouldn't die. And I made haste out of the wood, but I could hear it crying all the while; and when I got out into the fields, it was as if I was held fast—I couldn't go away, for all I wanted so to go. And I sat against the haystack to watch if anybody 'ud come: I was very hungry, and I'd only a bit of bread left; but I couldn't go away. And after ever such a while—hours and hours—the man came —him in a smock-frock, and he looked at me so. I was frightened, and I made haste and went on. I thought he was going to the wood, and would perhaps find the baby. And I went right on, till I came to a village, a long way off from the wood; and I was very sick, and faint, and hungry. I got something to eat there, and bought a loaf. But I was frightened to stay. I heard the baby crying, and thought the other folks heard it too,—and I went on. But I was so tired, and it was getting towards dark. And at last, by the roadside there was a barn— ever such a way off any house—like the barn in Abbot's Close; and I thought I could go in there and hide myself among the hay and straw, and nobody 'ud be likely to come. I went in, and it was half full o' trusses of straw, and there was some hay, too. And I made myself a bed, ever so far behind, where nobody could find me; and I was so tired and weak, I went to sleep ... But oh, the baby's crying kept waking me; and I thought that man as looked at me so was come and laying hold of me. But I must have slept a long while at last, though I didn't know; for when I got up and went out of the barn, I didn't know whether it was night or morning. But it was morning, for it kept getting lighter; and I turned back the way I'd come. I couldn't help it, Dinah; it was the baby's crying made me go: and yet I was frightened to death. I thought that man in the smock-frock 'ud see me, and know I put the baby there. But I went on, for all that: I'd left off thinking about going home—it had gone out o' my mind. I saw nothing but that place in the wood where I'd buried the baby...I see it now. O Dinah! Shall I allays see it?'

From *Adam Bede* by George Eliot, 1859

A different solution for a different kind of rejected woman . . .

JASON: You hateful thing, you woman most utterly loathed
    By the gods and me and by all the race of mankind,
    You who have had the heart to raise a sword against
    Your children, you, their mother, and left me childless,—
    You have done this, and do you still look at the sun
    And at the earth, after these most fearful doings?
    I wish you dead. Now I see it plain, though at that time
    I did not, when I took you from your foreign home
    And brought you to a Greek house, you, an evil thing,
    A traitress to your father and your native land.
    The gods hurled the avenging curse of yours on me.
    For your own brother you slew at your own hearthside,
    And them came aboard that beautiful ship, the Argo.
    And that was your beginning. When you were married
    To me, your husband, and had borne children to me,
    For the sake of pleasure in the bed you killed them.
    There is no Greek woman who would have dared such deeds,
    Out of all those whom I passed over and chose you
    To marry instead, a bitter destructive match,
    A monster, not a woman, having a nature
    Wilder than that of Scylla in the Tuscan sea.
    Ah! no, not if I had ten thousand words of shame
    Could I sting you. You are naturally so brazen.
    Go, worker in evil, stained with your children's blood.
    For me remains to cry aloud upon my fate,
    Who will get no pleasure from my new-wedded love,
    And the boys whom I begot and brought up, never
    Shall I speak to them alive. Oh, my life is over!
MEDEA: Long would be the answer which I might have made to
    These words of yours, if Zeus the father did not know
    How I have treated you and what you did to me.
    No, it was not to be that you should scorn my love,
    And pleasantly live your life through, laughing at me;

Nor would the princess, not he who offered the match,
Kreon, drive me away without paying for it.
So now you may call me a monster, if you wish,
O Scylla housed in the caves of the Tuscan sea
I too, as I had to, have taken hold of your heart.
JASON: You feel the pain yourself. You share in my sorrow.
MEDEA: Yes, and my grief is gain when you cannot mock it.

From *The Medea of Euripides*, fifth century BC,
translated from the Greek by Rex Warner

Alice contrives an accident, using a child as her instrument.

'Oh, but it is not nonsense,' the woman said. 'She was nearly five, a
child of five playing with a pistol she had taken from a drawer while
her mother slept. The pistol went off and Lily died. An accident, of
course, but Maurice was too sensitive a soul to bear the thought of her
growing up knowing that she had killed her mother. Besides, it was
likely that Maurice would have been convicted in any event. It was
known that he and I were intimate, he wanted his freedom from Lily;
and he was at the door of Lily's bedroom when the shot was fired. But
that was a slight matter to him: his one desire was to save the child
from the memory of what she had done, so her life might not be blackened by the knowledge that she had, however accidentally, killed her
mother.' What made this especially nasty was the niceness with which
the woman smiled as she talked, and the care—almost fastidious—
with which she selected her words, mouthing them daintily. She went
on: 'Gabrielle was always, even before she became addicted to drugs,
a child of, one might say, limited mentality; and so, by the time the
London police had found us, we had succeeded in quite emptying her
mind of the last trace of memory. This is, I assure you, the entire truth.
She killed her mother; and her father, to use your expression, took the
fall for her.'

'Fairly plausible,' I conceded, 'but it doesn't hang together right.

There's a chance that you made Leggett believe that, but I doubt it. I think you're trying to hurt your stepdaughter because she's told us of seeing you knife Ruppert downstairs.'

She pulled her lips back from her teeth and took a quick step toward me, her eyes wide and white-ringed; then she checked herself, laughed sharply, and the glare went from her eyes—or maybe went back through them, to smoulder behind them. She put her hand on her hips and smiled playfully, airily, at me and spoke playfully to me, while mad hatred glowed behind eyes, smile, and voice. 'Am I? Then I must tell you this, which I should not tell you unless it was true. I taught her to kill her mother. Do you understand? I taught her, trained her, drilled her, rehearsed her. Do you understand that? Lily and I were true sisters, inseparable, hating one another poisonously. Maurice, he wished to marry neither of us—why should he?— though he was intimate enough with both. You are to try to understand that literally. But we were poverty-ridden and he was not, and because we were and he wasn't, Lily wished to marry him. And I, I wished to marry him because she did. We were true sisters, like that in all things. But Lily got him, first—trapped him—that is crude but exact—into matrimony. Gabrielle was born six or seven months later. What a happy little family we were. I lived with them—weren't Lily and I inseparable?—and from the first Gabrielle had more love for me than for her mother. I saw to that: there was nothing her Aunt Alice wouldn't do for her dear niece; because her preferring me infuriated Lily, not that Lily herself loved the child so much, but that we were sisters; and whatever one wanted the other wanted, not to share, but exclusively.

'Gabrielle had hardly been born before I began planning what I should some day do; and when she was nearly five I did it. Maurice's pistol, a small one, was kept in a locked drawer high in a chiffonier. I unlocked the drawer, unloaded the pistol and taught Gabrielle an amusing little game. I would lie on Lily's bed, pretending to sleep. The child would push a chair to the chiffonier, climb up on it, take the pistol from the drawer, creep over to the bed, put the muzzle of the pistol to my head, and press the trigger. When she did it well, making little or no noise, holding the pistol correctly in her tiny hands, I would reward her with candy, cautioning her against saying anything about the game to her mother or to anyone else, as we were going to surprise her mother with it. We did. We surprised her completely one afternoon when, having taken aspirin for a headache, Lily was sleeping in her bed. That time I unlocked the drawer but did not unload the pistol. Then I told the child she might play the game with her mother; and I went to visit friends on the floor below, so no one would think I had any part in my dear sister's demise . . .'

From *The Dain Curse* by Dashiell Hammett (1894–1961)

Brother murders brother out in the hayfield while their mother waits at home for her sons.

> 'Farewell to barn and stack and tree,
> Farewell to Severn shore.
> Terence, look your last at me,
> For I come home no more.
>
> 'The sun burns on the half-mown hill,
> By now the blood has dried;
> And Maurice amongst the hay lies still
> And my knife is in his side.
>
> 'My mother thinks us long away;
> 'Tis time the field were mown.
> She had two sons at rising day,
> To-night she'll be alone.
>
> 'And here's a bloody hand to shake,
> And oh, man, here's good-bye;
> We'll sweat no more on scythe and rake,
> My bloody hands and I.

'I wish you strength to bring you pride,
And a love to keep you clean,
And I wish you luck come Lammastide,
At racing on the green.

'Long for me the rick will wait,
And long will wait the fold,
And long will stand the empty plate,
And dinner will be cold.'

From *A Shropshire Lad* by A. E. Housman, 1896

Most common have been the killings of spouses by their husbands or wives or of lovers by their partners. Rojack has killed his wife in a jealous rage after she boasted to him of her infidelities. His immediate reaction is to go into the next room and make love to the German maid. Now he has to make Deborah's death look like an accident.

And I smiled in terror, for it was also the boldest choice. Was I brave enough? Something in me lingered back—I had a panicked minute of argument in which I tried to find some other way. Perhaps I could take Deborah to the elevator (my poor wife is drunk) or sneak her down the stairs, no, altogether impossible, and then I sighed: if I missed on this one, it was the electric chair for sure, I had a wistful sadness now I had not tried to cast a baby into Ruta—she might be the last woman for me—and then I stood up from my seat, went to look at Deborah, knelt beside her again, and put my hand under her hips. Her bowels had voided. Suddenly I felt like a child, I was ready to weep. There was a stingy fish-like scent in the air, not unreminiscent of Ruta. They were mistress and maid and put their musk in opposite pockets. I hesitated, and since there was nothing to do but go on, I went to the bathroom, took some paper, and cleaned Deborah. It was a discipline to be thorough. Then I disposed of the waste, listening to the hound's sigh of the closet water, and came back to look out the open window. No. Not yet. First I turned off the brightest lights. Then in a panic of strength, like the desperation to get out of a burning room, I lifted her up, at what a cost I lifted her up, for her body was almost too heavy (or I was that empty with fright) and balanced her feet on the ledge, it was harder than I thought, and with a fever that no one see me at the open window now, not this instant, no, I took a breath and thrust her out and fell back myself to the carpet as if she had shoved me back, and lying there I counted to two, to three, how fast I do not know, feeling the weight of her flight like a thrill in my chest, and heard a sound come up from the pavement all ten stories below, a flat, surprisingly loud and hollow thump as car brakes screamed and metal went colliding into metal with that howl of a shape which is suddenly collapsed, and I stood up then and leaned out the window and looked and there was Deborah's body half beneath the front of a car and a pile-up of three or four behind and traffic screaming to a stall on back, all the way half a mile back, and I howled then in a simulation of woe, but the woe was real—for the first time I knew she was gone—and it was an animal howl.

One scalding wash of sorrow, and I felt clean. I went to the telephone, dialed 0, asked, 'What is the number of the police?' The operator said, 'Just a minute, I'll get it for you,' and I waited for eight long rings while my nerve teetered like a clown on a tightrope, and a cacophony rose up all ten stories from the ground. I heard my voice giving my name and Deborah's address to the mouthpiece, and that voice of mine then said, 'Get over here right away, will you. I can hardly talk, there's been a frightful accident.' I hung up, went to the door, and shouted down the stairs, 'Ruta, get dressed, get dressed quick. Mrs Rojack has killed herself.'

From *An American Dream* by Norman Mailer, 1965

And a husband who convinces himself that the kind of murder he contemplates is 'not murder at all'.

Of course, Dr Bickleigh did not think of what he proposed to do as 'murder' at all. Not that he consciously avoided the word. He simply could not accept it. Other people 'murdered' their wives, but other people's cases were quite different. His case was unique: Dr Bickleigh was quite sure of that. Julia was impossible; life with Julia any longer was impossible; divorce by consent was impossible, because Julia, having had her chance, had thrown it away, and Julia never changed her mind more than once; divorce in any case would be calamitous, from his professional standpoint; a future without Madeleine was unthinkable; only one course was inevitable. It was quite simple.

Dr Bickleigh did understand quite well that the world would call that course 'murder'; but how could the cloddish world ever understand the peculiar delicacy of his own feelings, or appreciate what Madeleine meant to him? Better that a thousand humdrum Julias should be sacrificed than that Madeleine should suffer a moment: Julia simply did not count compared with Madeleine: but how could the world ever understand that? Occasionally, in moments of surprised detachment, Dr Bickleigh did find himself on the world's side of the fence. 'By Jove, but it *is* murder.' But the thought was invariably followed by an odd little thrill of pride: 'Well, then, here's one murderer going to get away with it, anyhow.' And the next moment he would see that of course it was not murder at all.

His normal attitude was simplicity itself. In his duties he had put away plenty of pet animals who had passed their usefulness. Now the time had come to put Julia away. That was all.

From *Malice Aforethought* by Francis Iles, 1931

[16]

Another wife-murderer, finding himself bitterly remorseful, argues against punishment on the grounds that he has suffered enough.

The last words in court of the Moscow student Maukoff, who had murdered his wife, were as follows:

'She is dead, she is a martyr, perhaps by now she is a holy being; whereas I remain here below to carry, for the rest of my life, the heavy cross of crime and repentance. Why punish me, when I have already punished myself? I can still eat nice little apples and eggs, just as I did before, but they no longer possess their former, sweet flavour. Nothing gives me any joy now—why then punish me?'

From *Fragments from My Diary* by Maxim Gorky (1868–1936)

In 1857 Madeleine Smith was tried for the murder of her lover Emile L'Angelier by the administration of arsenic. The verdict, peculiar to Scottish law, was 'Not Proven', though most believed she was guilty. Four days later this girl, aged twenty-one, wrote to the matron of Edinburgh Prison.

Dear Miss Aitken,
You shall be glad to hear that I am well—in fact I am quite well, and my spirits are not in the least down. I left Edinburgh and went to Slateford, and got home to Rowaleyn during the night. But, alas, I found Mama in a bad state of health. But I trust in a short time all will be well with her. The others are all well. The feeling in the west is not so good towards me as you think Edinburgh people showed me. I rather think it shall be necessary for me to leave Scotland for a few months, but Mama is so unwell we do not like to fix anything at present. If ever you see Mr C. Combe, tell him that the panel was not at all pleased with the verdict. I was delighted with the loud

[17]

cheer the court gave. I did not feel in the least put about when the jury were out considering whether they would send me home or keep me. I think I must have had several hundred letters, all from gentlemen, some offering me consolation, and some their hearths and homes. My *friend* I know nothing of. I have not seen him. I hear he has been ill, which I don't much care. I hope you will give me a note. Thank Miss Bell and Agnes in my name for all their kindness and attention to me. I should like you to send me my Bible and watch to 124 Vincent Street, Glasgow, to J. Smith. The country is looking most lovely. As soon as I know my arrangements I shall let you know where I am to be sent to. With kind love to yourself and Mr Smith [*sic*], ever believe me, yours sincerely,

Madeleine Smith

From *The Trial of Madeleine Smith* by F. Tennyson Jesse, 1927

Alice, the wife of Arden of Feversham, plots with a servant to kill her husband so that she may be free to entertain her lover Mosbie. Michael is a sixteenth-century hit-man.

ALICE: I know he loves me well, but dares not come,
    Because my husband is so jealous,
    And these my narrow-prying neighbours blab,
    Hinder our meetings when we would confer.
    But, if I live, that block shall be removed,
    And, Mosbie, thou that comes to me by stealth,
    Shalt neither fear the biting speech of men
    Nor Arden's looks; as surely he shall die
    As I abhor him and love only thee.
    (*Here enters Michael.*)
    How now, Michael, whither are you going?

MICHAEL: To fetch my master's nag.
   I hope you'll think on me.
ALICE: Ay; but, Michael, see you keep your oath,
   And be as secret as you are resolute.
MICHAEL: I'll see he shall not live above a week.
ALICE: On that condition, Michael, here is my hand:
   None shall have Mosbie's sister but thyself.
MICHAEL: I understand the painter here hard by
   Hath made report that he and Sue is sure.
ALICE: There's no such matter, Michael; believe it not.
MICHAEL: But he hath sent a dagger sticking in a heart,
   With a verse or two stolen from a painted cloth,
   The which I hear the wench keeps in her chest.
   Well, let her keep it! I shall find a fellow
   That can both write and read and make rhyme too.
   And if I do—well, I say no more:
   I'll send from London such a taunting letter
   As she shall eat the heart he sent with salt
   And fling the dagger at the painter's head.
ALICE: What needs all this? I say that Susan's thine.
MICHAEL: Why, then I say that I will kill my master,
   Or anything that you will have me do.

From *Arden of Feversham*, author unknown, published 1592

Dr Crippen was hanged for the murder of his wife. In spite of dismembering the body and burying it under the floorboards of his house, he seems to have been far from the monster the public were led to think he was.

But the most amazing feature of the trial was the absolute coolness and imperturbability of Crippen in the long and terrible cross-examination which will be read in its place. The hideous moments in which the pieces of his dead wife's skin were handed round in a soup plate for inspection left him, alone of all the people in that crowded court, quite unmoved. He peered at them with an intelligent curiosity as though they had been mere museum specimens. Not by one word or tremor did this frail little man betray any sign of his terrible position, to which, nevertheless, as we know from other evidence, he was acutely and tragically sensitive. This behaviour characterised him up to his very last moments of life. And just as the Crown, with all its resources, had not been able to produce a single person who could say otherwise than that in every relationship of life Crippen had always behaved with kindness, consideration and unselfishness, so everyone who came in contact with him from his trial to his death—and some of them were fairly hardened prison officials—looked upon him not only with respect, but with something like affection.

He never gave any trouble, showed any concern, or asked for any benefit for himself; all his concern and all his requests were for the woman he loved. I have seen the tragic little book in which it was the duty of the warders who sat and watched with him day and night in the condemned cell to record his conduct from hour to hour, and although I do not feel myself free to quote from it, there is nothing in that record that shows any preoccupation whatever except anxiety on behalf of another. The only time he broke down was when, late on the night before his execution, the Governor of Pentonville Prison brought him a telegram of farewell from Miss Le Neve, and his one request, when the Governor at this same midnight interview asked him if there was anything he could possibly do for him, was that the one or two letters that he had received from her, and her photograph, should be buried in the prison grave with him on the morrow. This promise was given and kept.

. . . We may consider Crippen a hateful man; but nobody who came in contact with him was able to say so. From those who, whether in business relations or as friends of his wife, had no reason to like or praise him, to the officials of the prison in which he was executed as a condemned murderer, there is but one chorus of testimony to his character as tested by daily intercourse with his fellow-men; even in regard to the very circumstances surrounding his crime, or at any rate following it, there is the same extraordinary feature; the very crime itself brought out in him high human qualities.

From *The Trial of Dr Hawley Harvey Crippen* by Filson Young, 1920

The light put out for ever . . .

OTHELLO: It is the cause, it is the cause, my soul.
   Let me not name it to you, you chaste stars.
   It is the cause. Yet I'll not shed her blood,
   Nor scar that whiter skin of hers than snow,
   And smooth as monumental alabaster.
   Yet she must die, else she'll betray more men.
   Put out the light, and then put out the light.
   If I quench thee, thou flaming minister,
   I can again thy former light restore,
   Should I repent me; but once put out thy light,
   Thou cunning'st pattern of excelling nature,
   I know not where is that Promethean heat
   That can thy light relume. When I have pluck'd thy rose,
   I cannot give it vital growth again;
   It needs must wither. I'll smell thee on the tree.
   (*He kisses her.*)
   O balmy breath, that dost almost persuade
   Justice to break her sword. One more, one more!

Be thus when thou art dead, and I will kill thee,
And love thee after. One more, and that's the last!
So sweet was ne'er so fatal. I must weep,
But they are cruel tears. This sorrow's heavenly;
It strikes where it doth love.

From *Othello, the Moor of Venice* by William Shakespeare, 1604

In this poem Hardy at his most curious tells of an unparalleled murder method and the workings of an extraordinary woman's mind. She is relating her experience to the dead man's successor.

'Still, dear, it is incredible to me
　　That here, alone,
You should have sewed him up until he died,
And in this very bed. I do not see
How you could do it, seeing what might betide.'

'Well, he came home one midnight, liquored deep—
　　Worse than I'd known—
And lay down heavily, and soundly slept:
Then, desperate driven, I thought of it, to keep
Him from me when he woke. Being an adept

'With needle and thimble, as he snored, click-click
　　An hour I'd sewn,
Till, had he roused up, he couldn't have moved from bed,
So tightly laced in sheet and quilt and tick
He lay. And in the morning he was dead.

'Ere people came I drew the stitches out,
　　And thus it was shown
To be a stroke.'—'It's a strange tale!,' said he.
'And this same bed?'—'Yes, here it came about.'
'Well, it sounds strange—told here and now to me.

'Did you intend his death by your tight lacing?'
  'Oh, that I cannot own.
I could not think of else that would avail
When he should wake up and attempt embracing.'—
'Well, it's a cool queer tale!'

From 'Her Second Husband Hears Her Story'
by Thomas Hardy, 1928

The state of mind in which a pair of lovers spur each other on to commit murder has been named folie à deux.

He stepped out of the bedroom into the hall. He had never known it so quiet. He did not bother with the light. There was just enough of a moon to give a colourless light, although he was not sure quite how moonlight was penetrating here. He went to the kitchen and found a sharp knife. He went back in the hall and knelt by the cases and unfastened the straps on both. Then he opened one of them. The parts were neatly in place, just as Maria had packed them. He lifted out a piece and cut away the waterproof material and laid an arm gently down on the carpet. There was no unpleasant smell, he was not too late. He pushed the wrapping well away to one side, and then he set about freeing a leg, a thigh, and the chest. There was surprisingly little blood, and besides, the carpet was red. He set the pieces down on the hall carpet in their correct positions. The human shape was resuming. He opened the second case and unwrapped the lower body and the limbs. It was therefore before him, a headless body lying on its back. He had the head in his hands now. He turned it and saw through the material the outline of the nose and the imprecise features of the face.

It was while he was using the point of the knife to prise away the glued seam that he saw something that caught his attention. He was holding the heavy head down on the floor but he could no longer move the knife. It was not the prospect of seeing Otto's face. Nor was it the completed figure lying on the carpet next to him. What he had seen was the bedroom wall and his bed. He had forced his eyes open a fraction and seen the shape of his own body under the blankets. For two seconds he had heard the traffic in the street outside, still late night traffic, and he had seen his own immovable body. Then his eyes shut, and he was back here, with the knife in his hand, picking away again at the fabric.

It worried him to know that what was so real was a dream. It meant that anything could happen. There were no rules. He was putting Otto back together, undoing the day's work. He was peeling away a layer of rubberised cloth, and here was the side of the head, with the top of an ear visible. He ought to stop himself, he thought, he ought to wake before Otto came to life. With an effort he opened his eyes again. He saw a part of a hand and an impression of his feet under the blanket. If he could move just one part of himself, or make a sound, the tiniest of sounds, he could bring himself back. But the body he occupied was inert. He was trying to move his toe. He could hear a motorbike in the street outside. If someone would come in the room and touch him. He was trying to shout. He could not part his lips or fill his lungs. His eyes were weighing down, and he was in the hall once more.

Why was the material sticking to the side of Otto's face? It was the bite of course, the blood from his cheek had congealed on the cloth. That was only one reason why Otto was going to punish him. He pulled the cloth and it came away with a rasping sound. The rest was easy. It fell away and the bare head was in his hands. The eyes with the drunk's red rims were watching him, waiting. It was simply a matter of lifting the head on to the torn neck, then it could begin again. He should have been kept divided up but now it was too late. Even before the head was properly in place, the hands were reaching for the knife. Otto was sitting up. He could see the empty cases, and the knife was in his hand. Leonard knelt in front of him and tipped back his head to offer up his throat. Otto would make a swift job. He would have to pack the cases himself. He would carry Leonard to the Zoo station. Otto was a Berliner, he was an old drinking friend of the admiral.

Here was the bedroom wall again, the blanket, the edge of the sheet, the pillow. His body was lead. Otto would never carry him alone. Piper McTaggart would help. Leonard tried half-heartedly for a scream. It was better that it should happen. He heard the air pass between his teeth. He tried to bend his leg. His eyes were closing again and he was going to die. His head moved, it turned an inch or so to one side. His cheek touched the pillow, and the touch unlocked all touch and he felt the weight of the blanket on his foot. His eyes were open and he could move his hand. He could shout. He was sitting up and reaching for the light switch.

Even with the light on, the dream was still there, waiting for him to return. He slapped his face and stood. His legs were weak, his eyes still wanted to close. He went into the bathroom and splashed water over his face. When he came out he turned on the hall light. The unopened cases were by the door.

From *The Innocent* by Ian McEwan, 1990

Remembered as The Brides in the Bath murderer, George Joseph Smith married a succession of young women and drowned them in order to secure the money for which he had insured their lives.

Smith took Bessie from town to town while he made official enquiries about how he might legally get possession of her fortune. In May they were in Herne Bay, renting a small house at 80 High Street, which had neither bathroom nor bath. On 2 July Smith heard from his lawyer that if he and Bessie both made wills and she died, he would inherit everything. The information signed her death-warrant. This time he had to kill his bride in order to get hold of her money and he had to act quickly, in case her relatives altered the terms of the settlement on her. Wills were drawn up and attested on 8 July.

The next day Smith bought a zinc bath (without taps) from an iron-monger, beating down the asking price of £2 to £1 17s 6d. In fact he never paid for it, returning the bath six days later, its purpose served.

On Wednesday, 10 July, he took his wife to a young newly qualified doctor called French, alleging she had had a fit. All Bessie Mun-
day complained of was a headache. At 1.30 am on the Friday, Dr
French was summoned to 80 High Street—Bessie had apparently had
another fit. She was in bed. He found nothing amiss: she looked as if
she had just woken up, was flushed and heavy-headed—it was a very
warm night. The doctor prescribed a sedative … That night, evidently
on Smith's instructions, she penned a letter to her uncle:

> Last Tuesday night I had a bad fit, and one again on Thursday night.
> My husband has been extremely kind and done all he could for me. He
> has provided me with the attention of the best medical men here, who
> are … visiting me day and night … My husband has strictly advised me
> to let all my relatives know of my breakdown. I have made out my
> will and left all to my husband. That is only natural, as I love my
> husband . . .

. . . The following morning, about 7.30, she prepared to have a
bath in a spare room, making about twenty journeys up and down
the stairs with a bucket to and from the kitchen, while Smith went
out to buy some fish. She got in the bath, her hair in curling-pins.
Smith returned.

From 'George Smith, The Murder of Bessie Mundy, 1912' in *The Murders of the
Black Museum 1870–1970* by Gordon Honeycombe, 1982

Murder for love sometimes destroys love . . .

When she got to my car she stopped and I got out. We didn't kiss. We didn't even say good-bye. I got out of her car, got in mine, started, and drove home.

When I got home, I looked at the clock. It was 10.25. I opened the bell box of the telephone. The card was still there. I closed the box and dropped the card in my pocket. I went in the kitchen and looked at the doorbell. That card was still there. I dropped it in my pocket. I went upstairs, ripped off my clothes, and got into pyjamas and slippers. I cut the bandage off my foot. I went down, shoved the bandage and cards into the fireplace, with a newspaper, and lit it. I watched it burn. Then I went to the telephone and started to dial. I still had one call-back to get, to round out the late part of my alibi. I felt something like a drawstring pull in my throat, and a sob popped out of me. I clapped the phone down. It was getting me. I knew I had to get myself under some kind of control. I swallowed a couple of times. I wanted to make sure of my voice, that it would sound OK. A dumb idea came to me that maybe if I would sing something, that would make me snap out of it. I started to sing 'The Isle of Capri'. I sang about two notes, and it swallowed into a kind of wail.

I went into the dining room and took a drink. I took another drink. I started mumbling to myself, trying to get so I could talk. I had to have something to mumble. I thought of the Lord's Prayer. I mumbled that a couple of times. I tried to mumble it another time, and couldn't remember how it went.

When I thought I could talk, I dialled again. It was 10.48. I dialled Ike Schwartz, that's another salesman with General.

'Ike, do me a favour, will you? I'm trying to figure out a proposition on a public liability bond for a wine company to have it ready for them tomorrow morning, and I'm going nuts. I came off without my rate book. Joe Pete can't find it, and I'm wondering if you'll look up what I want in yours. You got it with you?'

'Sure, I'll be glad to.'

I gave him the dope. He said give him fifteen minutes and he'd call back.

I walked around, digging my fingernails into my hands, trying to hold on to myself. The drawstring began to jerk on my throat again. I began mumbling again, saying over and over what I had just said to Ike. The phone rang. I answered. He had it figured for me, he said, and began to give it to me. He gave it to me three different ways, so I'd have it all. It took him twenty minutes. I took it down, what he said. I could feel the sweat squeezing out on my forehead and running down off my nose. After a while he was done.

'OK, Ike, that's just what I wanted to know. That's just how I wanted it. Thanks a thousand times.'

Soon as he hung up everything cracked. I dived for the bathroom. I was sicker than I had ever been in my life. After that passed I fell into bed. It was a long time before I could turn out the light. Then I lay there staring into the dark. Every now and then I would have a chill or something and start to tremble. Then that passed and I lay there, like a dope. Then I started to think. I tried not to, but it would creep up on me. I knew then what I had done. I had killed a man. I had killed a man to get a woman. I had put myself in her power, so there was one person in the world that could point a finger at me, and I would have to die. I had done all that for her, and I never wanted to see her again as long as I lived.

That's all it takes, one drop of fear, to curdle love into hate.

From *Double Indemnity* by James M. Cain, 1943

Paul is to be executed for the murder of his wife. In the condemned cell he still worries about what people will think of him.

And in his cell Paul lay on his bed; and his two warders sat at the table, silent, unhappy. Paul thought of his childhood, and of his father and mother whom he would never see again, and of the river in Clissold Park and the dead leaves and the blossom, and of Myra. And he thought often and often, 'It is done quickly. Probably one second of excruciating pain, and it's all over. I can hold myself together for that.' He tried to picture what he would see in the execution room, his last view of the world; and he rehearsed his last words. He turned in his bed, but not too often, because he wanted the warders to think him a 'good patient, who bore up well'. Sometimes he waited a long time before allowing himself to turn. Sweat formed on his brow and slipped to the pillow, as if the cell, with its dim light burning, were unusually warm, but he waited before brushing it away or throwing back the clothes; because dignity sat ill with restlessness. But why, he asked himself, did he worry any more about what people thought of him? Soon he would be done for ever with the world. Done with it, and what then? He had made his effort at faith, asked forgiveness for his fearful sin, and if all the chaplain said was true, he would pass into God's peace. In a few hours. Peace. Why, if this were true, surely he ought to be almost happy! And if it were not true, well, he must just shrug his shoulders, and then square them to the senseless burden of life. A burden and a blow, and all would be over. Peace in either event. And in either event he must finish well—oh, yes, yes! This vanity, or this pride, was with one to the last, stepping like a faithful friend on to the execution platform at one's side, and standing under the beam. He must show a lifted head and a steady lip. 'It is done quickly. Twenty seconds from cell door to scaffold; and one second of pain. I can hold myself in control for that half minute. I'll not show fear.' To steady himself for the great moment he repeated it a thousand times as the night wore away. 'I'll not show fear.'

From *We, the Accused* by Ernest Raymond, 1935

[29]

2

'THE WAY OF HIS WICKEDNESS'

Murder for Revenge

Henry Thorne had already heard of, and already seen, Mary Scatcherd; but hitherto she had not fallen in the way of his wickedness. Now, however, when he heard that she was to be decently married, the devil tempted him to tempt her. It boots not to tell all the tale. It came out clearly enough when all was told, that he made her most distinct promises of marriage; he even gave her such in writing; and having in this way obtained from her her company during some of her little holidays—her Sundays or summer evenings—he seduced her. Scatcherd accused him openly of having intoxicated her with drugs; and Thomas Thorne, who took up the case, ultimately believed the charge. It became known in Barchester that she was with child, and that the seducer was Henry Thorne.

Roger Scatcherd, when the news first reached him, filled himself with drink, and then swore that he would kill them both. With manly wrath, however, he set forth first against the man, and that with manly weapons. He took nothing with him but his fists and a big stick as he went in search of Henry Thorne.

The two brothers were then lodging together at a farm-house close abutting on the town. This was not an eligible abode for a medical practitioner; but the young doctor had not been able to settle himself eligibly since his father's death; and wishing to put what constraint he could upon his brother, had so located himself. To this farm-house came Roger Scatcherd one sultry summer evening, his anger gleaming from his blood-shot eyes, and his rage heightened to madness by the rapid pace at which he had run from the city, and by the ardent spirits which were fermenting within him.

At the very gate of the farm-yard, standing placidly with his cigar in his mouth, he encountered Henry Thorne. He had thought of searching for him through the whole premises, of demanding his victim with loud exclamations, and making his way to him through all obstacles. In lieu of that, there stood the man before him.

'Well, Roger, what's in the wind?' said Henry Thorne.

They were the last words he ever spoke.

From *Doctor Thorne* by Anthony Trollope, 1858

The Vicario brothers decide to avenge their sister's honour. On her wedding night, her husband has discovered that she has lost her virginity to her former lover, Santiago Nasar.

Clotilde Armenta hadn't finished dispensing her milk when the Vicario brothers returned with two other knives wrapped up in newspapers. One was for quartering, with a strong, rusty blade twelve inches long and three inches wide, which had been put together by Pedro Vicario with the metal from the marquetry saw at a time when German knives were no longer available because of the war. The other one was shorter, but broad and curved. The investigator had made sketches of them in the brief, perhaps because he had trouble describing them, and all he ventured to say was that it looked like a miniature scimitar. It was with these knives that the crime was committed, and both were rudimentary and had seen a lot of use.

Faustino Santos couldn't understand what had happened. 'They came to sharpen their knives a second time,' he told me, 'and once more they shouted for people to hear they were going to cut Santiago Nasar's guts out, so I thought they were kidding around, especially since I didn't pay any attention to the knives and thought they were the same ones.' This time, however, Clotilde Armenta noticed from the time she saw them enter that they didn't have the same determination as before.

Actually, they'd had their first disagreement. Not only were they much more different inside than they looked on the outside, but in difficult emergencies they showed opposite characters. We, their friends, had spotted it ever since grammar school. Pablo Vicario was six minutes older than his brother, and he was the more imaginative and resolute since adolescence. Pedro Vicario always seemed more sentimental to me, and by the same token more authoritarian. They presented themselves together for military service at the age of twenty, and Pablo Vicario was excused in order to stay home and take care of the family. Pedro Vicario served for eleven months on police patrol. The army routine, aggravated by the fear of death, had matured his tendency to command and the habit of deciding for his brother. He also came back with a case of sergeant's blennorrhagia that resisted the most brutal methods of military medicine as well as the arsenic injections and permanganate purges of Dr Dionisio Iguarán. Only in jail did they manage to cure it. We, his friends, agreed that Pablo Vicario had suddenly developed the strange dependence of a younger brother when Pedro Vicario returned with a barrack-room soul and with the novel trick of lifting his shirt for anyone who wanted to see a bullet wound with seton on his left side. He even began to develop a kind of fervour over the great man's blennorrhagia that his brother wore like a war medal.

Pedro Vicario, according to his own declaration, was the one who made the decision to kill Santiago Nasar, and at first his brother only followed along. But he was also the one who considered his duty fulfilled when the mayor disarmed them, and then it was Pablo Vicario who assumed command. Neither of the two mentioned that disagreement in their separate statements to the investigator. But Pablo Vicario confirmed several times to me that it hadn't been easy for him to convince his brother about their final resolve. Maybe it was really nothing but a wave of panic, but the fact is that Pablo Vicario went into the pigsty alone to get the other two knives, while his brother agonised, drop by drop, trying to urinate under the tamarind trees. 'My brother never knew what it was like,' Pedro Vicario told me in our only interview. 'It was like pissing ground glass.' Pablo Vicario found him hugging the tree when he came back with the knives. 'He was in a cold sweat from the pain,' he told me, 'and he tried to tell me to go on by

[35]

myself because he was in no condition to kill anybody.' He sat down on one of the carpenters' benches they'd set up under the trees for the wedding lunch, and he dropped his pants down to his knees. 'He spent about half an hour changing the gauze he had his prick wrapped in,' Pablo Vicario told me. Actually, he hadn't delayed more than ten minutes, but it was something so difficult and puzzling for Pablo Vicario that he interpreted it as some new trick on his brother's part to waste time until dawn. So he put the knife in his hand and dragged him off almost by force in search of their sister's lost honour.

'There's no way out of this,' he told him. 'It's as if it had already happened.'

They left by way of the pigpen gate with the knives unwrapped, pursued by the uproar of the dogs in the yards. It was beginning to get light. 'It wasn't raining,' Pablo Vicario remembered. 'Just the opposite,' Pedro recalled. 'There was a sea wind and you could still count the stars with your finger.' The news had been so well spread by then that Hortensia Baute opened her door precisely as they were passing her house, and she was the first to weep for Santiago Nasar. 'I thought they'd already killed him,' she told me, 'because I saw the knives in the light from the street lamp and it looked to me that they were dripping blood.' One of the few houses open on that misplaced street was that of Prudencia Cotes, Pablo Vicario's fiancée. Whenever the twins passed by there at that time, and especially on Fridays when they were going to the market, they would go in to have their first cup of coffee. They pushed open the door to the courtyard, surrounded by the dogs, who recognised them in the half-light of dawn, and they greeted Prudencia Cotes's mother in the kitchen. Coffee wasn't ready yet.

'We'll leave it for later,' Pablo Vicario said. 'We're in a hurry now.'

'I can imagine, my sons,' she said. 'Honour doesn't wait.'

From *Chronicle of a Death Foretold* by Gabriel García Márquez, 1986, translated from the Spanish by Gregory Rabassa

The sense that his revenge has been inadequate makes a murderer long to pursue his victim beyond the grave.

In the Papal State there is a law by which no criminal may be led to his death before he has received absolution. This Piachi, when his life had been declared forfeit, stubbornly refused to do. After all the arguments of religion had been vainly adduced to convince him of the heinousness of his behaviour, he was led out to the gallows in the hope that the sight of the death that awaited him might frighten him into penitence. On one side stood a priest who in a voice like the last trump described to him all the terrors of hell into which his soul was about to be plunged; opposite stood another, holding in his hand the Body of Christ, the sacred means of redemption, and spoke to him of the glorious abodes of eternal peace. 'Will you accept the blessed gift of salvation?' they both asked him. 'Will you receive the sacrament?' 'No,' replied Piachi. 'Why not?' 'I do not want to be saved, I want to go down into the deepest pit of hell, I want to find Nicolo again—for he will not be in heaven—and continue my vengeance on him which I could not finish here to my full satisfaction.' And so saying he ascended the ladder and called upon the hangman to perform his duty. In the end the execution had to be stayed and the wretched man taken back to prison, for the law protected him. On three successive days similar attempts were made and every time without avail. On the third day, forced once more to come down from the latter unhanged, he raised his fists in a gesture of bitter rage and cursed the inhuman law that forbade him to go to hell. He called upon the whole legion of devils to come and fetch him, swore he had no other wish but to be doomed and damned, and vowed he would throttle the first priest who came to hand if by so doing he might get to hell and lay hold of Nicolo again! When this was reported to the Pope, he ordered that Piachi should be executed without absolution; and unaccompanied by any priest, he was strung up very quietly in the Piazza del Popolo.

From 'The Foundling' by Heinrich von Kleist (1777–1811), translated from the German by David Luke and Nigel Reeves

[37]

Verloc, the secret agent, has attempted to blow up Greenwich Obser-vatory, but it is his wife's brother, the brain-damaged Stevie, who has been the victim of the bomb.

'I wish to goodness,' he growled, huskily, 'I had never seen Green-wich Park or anything belonging to it.'

The veiled sound filled the small room with its moderate volume, well adapted to the modest nature of the wish. The waves of air of the proper length, propagated in accordance with correct mathematical formulas, flowed around all the inanimate things in the room, lapped against Mrs Verloc's head as if it had been a head of stone. And incredible as it may appear, the eyes of Mrs Verloc seemed to grow still larger. The audible wish of Mr Verloc's overflowing heart flowed into an empty place in his wife's memory. Greenwich Park. A park! That's where the boy was killed. A park—smashed branches, torn leaves, gravel, bits of brotherly flesh and bone, all spouting up together in the manner of a firework. She remembered now what she had heard, and she remembered it pictorially. They had to gather him up with the shovel. Trembling all over with irrepressible shudders, she saw before her the very implement with its ghastly load scraped up from the ground. Mrs Verloc closed her eyes desperately, throwing upon that vision the night of her eyelids, where after a rainlike fall of mangled limbs the decapitated head of Stevie lingered suspended alone, and fading out slowly like the last star of a pyrotechnic display. Mrs Verloc opened her eyes.

Her face was no longer stony. Anybody could have noted the subtle change on her features, in the stare of her eyes, giving her a new and startled expression; an expression seldom observed by competent per-sons under the conditions of leisure and security demanded for thor-ough analysis, but whose meaning could not be mistaken at a glance. Mrs Verloc's doubts as to the end of the bargain no longer existed; her wits, no longer disconnected, were working under the control of her will. But Mr Verloc observed nothing. He was reposing in that pathetic condition of optimism induced by excess of fatigue. He did not want any more trouble—with his wife, too—of all people in the world. He had been unanswerable in his vindication. He was loved for himself. The present phase of her silence he interpreted favourably. This was the time to make it up with her. The silence had lasted long enough. He broke it calling to her in an undertone:

'Winnie.'

'Yes,' answered obediently Mrs Verloc the free woman. She commanded her wits now, her vocal organs; she felt herself to be in an almost preternaturally perfect control of every fibre of her body. It was all her own, because the bargain was at an end. She was clear sighted. She had become cunning. She chose to answer him so readily for a purpose. She did not wish that man to change his position on the sofa which was very suitable to the circumstances. She succeeded. The man did not stir. But after answering him she remained leaning negligently against the mantelpiece in the attitude of a resting wayfarer. She was unhurried. Her brow was smooth. The head and shoulders of Mr Verloc were hidden from her by the high side of the sofa. She kept her eyes fixed on his feet.

She remained thus mysteriously still and suddenly collected till Mr Verloc was heard with an accent of marital authority, and moving slightly to make room for her to sit on the edge of the sofa.

'Come here,' he said in a peculiar tone, which might have been the tone of brutality, but was intimately known to Mrs Verloc as the note of wooing.

She started forward at once, as if she were still a loyal woman, bound to that man by an unbroken contract. Her right hand skimmed slightly the edge of the table, and when she had passed on towards the sofa the carving knife had vanished without the slightest sound from the side of the dish. Mr Verloc heard the creaky plank in the floor, and was content. He waited. Mrs Verloc was coming. As if the homeless soul of Stevie had flown for shelter straight to the breast of his sister, guardian and protector, the resemblance of her face to that of her brother grew at every step, even to the droop of his lower lip, even to the slight divergence of the eyes. But Mr Verloc did not see that. He was lying on his back and staring upwards. He saw partly on the ceiling and partly on the wall the moving shadow of an arm with a clenched hand holding a carving knife. It flickered up and down. Its movements were leisurely. They were leisurely enough for Mr Verloc to recognise the limb and the weapon.

They were leisurely enough for him to take in the full meaning of the portent, and to taste the flavour of death rising in his gorge...

From *The Secret Agent* by Joseph Conrad, 1907

A mistreated wife takes revenge for a death.

'Mrs Peters!'

'Yes, Mrs Hale?'

'Do you think she—did it?'

Mrs Peters looked frightened. 'Oh, I don't know,' she said, in a voice that seemed to shrink from the subject.

'Well, I don't think she did,' affirmed Mrs Hale. 'Asking for an apron, and her little shawl. Worryin' about her fruit.'

'Mr Peters says . . .' Footsteps were heard in the room above; she stopped, looked up, then went on in a lowered voice: 'Mr Peters says —it looks bad for her. Mr Henderson is awful sarcastic in a speech, and he's going to make fun of her saying she didn't wake up.'

For a moment Mrs Hale had no answer. Then, 'Well, I guess John Wright didn't wake up—when they was slipping that rope under his neck,' she muttered.

'No, it's *strange*,' breathed Mrs Peters. 'They think it was such a—funny way to kill a man.'

'That's just what Mr Hale said,' said Mrs Hale, in a resolutely natural voice. 'There was a gun in the house. He says that's what he can't understand.'

'Mr Henderson said, coming out, that what was needed for the case was a motive. Something to show anger—or sudden feeling.'

'Well, I don't see any signs of anger around here,' said Mrs Hale. 'I don't . . .'

She stopped. Her eye was caught by a dish-towel in the middle of

[40]

the kitchen table. Slowly she moved towards the table. One half of it was wiped clean, the other half untidy. Her eyes made a slow, almost unwilling turn to the bucket of sugar and the half-empty bag beside it. Things begun—and not finished . . .

'Here's a bird-cage,' Mrs Peters said. 'Did she have a bird, Mrs Hale?'

'Why, I don't know whether she did or not.' She turned to look at the cage Mrs Peters was holding up. 'I've not been here in so long.' She sighed. 'There was a man round last year selling canaries cheap —but I don't know as she took one. Maybe she did. She used to sing real pretty herself.'

'Seems kind of funny to think of a bird in here. But she must have had one—or why would she have a cage? I wonder what happened to it.'

'I suppose maybe the cat got it,' suggested Mrs Hale, resuming her sewing.

'No; she didn't have a cat. She's got that feeling some people have about cats—being afraid of them. When they brought her to our house yesterday, my cat got into the room, and she was real upset and asked me to take it out.'

'My sister Bessie was like that,' laughed Mrs Hale.

The sheriff's wife did not reply. The silence made Mrs Hale turn. Mrs Peters was examining the bird-cage.

'Look at this door,' she said slowly. 'It's broke. One hinge has been pulled apart.'

Mrs Hale came nearer.

'Looks as if someone must have been—rough with it.'

Again their eyes met—startled, questioning, apprehensive. For a moment neither spoke nor stirred. Then Mrs Hale, turning away, said brusquely, 'If they're going to find any evidence, I wish they'd be about it. I don't like this place.'

'But I'm awful glad you came with me, Mrs Hale.' Mrs Peters put the bird-cage on the table and sat down. 'It would be lonesome for me —sitting here alone.'

'Yes, it would, wouldn't it?' agreed Mrs Hale. She had picked up

[41]

the sewing, but now it dropped to her lap, and she murmured: 'But I tell you what I *do* wish, Mrs Peters. I wish I had come over sometimes when she was here. I wish—I had.'

'But of course you were awful busy, Mrs Hale. Your house—and your children.'

'I could've come. I stayed away because it weren't cheerful—and that's why I ought to have come. I'—she looked around—'I've never liked this place. Maybe because it's down in a hollow and you don't see the road. I don't know what it is, but it's a lonesome place, and always was. I wish I had come over to see Minnie Foster sometimes. I can see now . . .'

'Well, you mustn't reproach yourself. Somehow we just don't see how it is with other folks till—something comes up.'

'Not having children makes less work,' mused Mrs Hale, 'but it makes a quiet house. And Wright out to work all day—and no company when he did come in. Did you know John Wright, Mrs Peters?'

'Not to know him. I've seen him in town. They say he was a good man.'

'Yes—good,' conceded John Wright's neighbour grimly. 'He didn't drink, and kept his word as well as most, I guess, and paid his debts. But he was a hard man, Mrs Peters. Just to pass the time of day with him . . .' She shivered. 'Like a raw wind that gets to the bone.' Her eye fell upon the cage on the table before her, and she added, 'I should think she would've wanted a bird!'

Suddenly she leaned forward, looking intently at the cage. 'But what do you s'pose went wrong with it?'

'I don't know,' returned Mrs Peters; 'unless it got sick and died.'

But after she said this she reached over and swung the broken door. Both women watched it.

'You didn't know—her?' Mrs Hale asked.

'Not till they brought her yesterday,' said the sheriff's wife.

'She—come to think of it, she was kind of like a bird herself. Real sweet and pretty, but kind of timid and—flutterly. How—she—did—change!'

Finally, as if struck with a happy thought and relieved to get back to everyday things: 'Tell you what, Mrs Peters, why don't you take the quilt in with you? It might take up her mind.'

'Why, I think that's a real nice idea, Mrs Hale. There couldn't possibly be any objection to that, could there? Now, just what will I take? I wonder if her patches are in here?' They turned to the sewing basket.

'Here's some red,' said Mrs Hale, bringing out a roll of cloth. Underneath this was a box. 'Here, maybe her scissors are in here—and her things.' She held it up. 'What a pretty box! I'll warrant that was something she had a long time ago—when she was a girl.'

She held it in her hand a moment; then, with a little sigh, opened it. Instantly her hand went to her nose. 'Why!'

Mrs Peters drew nearer—then turned away.

'There's something wrapped up in this piece of silk,' faltered Mrs Hale.

'This isn't scissors,' said Mrs Peters, in a shrinking voice.

Mrs Hale raised the piece of silk. 'Oh, Mrs Peters!' she cried. 'It's...'

Mrs Peters bent closer.

'It's the bird,' she whispered.

'But, Mrs Peters!' cried Mrs Hale. '*Look* at it! Its *neck*—look at its neck! It's all—other side *to.*'

The sheriff's wife again bent closer.

'Somebody wrung its neck,' said she, in a voice that was slow and deep.

From 'A Jury of Her Peers' by Susan Glaspell, 1917

[43]

Not her young husband but the man who first took Lolita from him has been Humbert Humbert's victim. Reviewing his past, he believes he has disregarded all the laws of humanity.

I wondered idly if some surgeon of genius might not alter his own career, and perhaps the whole destiny of mankind, by reviving quilted Quilty, Clare Obscure. Not that I cared; on the whole I wished to forget the whole mess—and when I did learn he was dead, the only satisfaction it gave me was the relief of knowing I need not mentally accompany for months a painful and disgusting convalescence interrupted by all kinds of unmentionable operations and relapses, and perhaps an actual visit from him, with trouble on my part to rationalise him as not being a ghost. Thomas had something. It was strange that the tactile sense, which is so infinitely less precious to men than sight, becomes at critical moments our main, if not only, handle to reality. I was all covered with Quilty—with the feel of that tumble before the bleeding.

The road now stretched across open country, and it occurred to me —not by way of protest, not as a symbol, or anything like that, but merely as a novel experience—that since I had disregarded all laws of humanity, I might as well disregard the laws of traffic. So I crossed to the left side of the highway and checked the feeling, and the feeling was good. It was a pleasant diaphragmal melting, with elements of diffused tactility, all this enhanced by the thought that nothing could be nearer to the elimination of basic physical laws than deliberately driving on the wrong side of the road. In a way, it was a very spiritual itch. Gently, dreamily, not exceeding twenty miles an hour, I drove on the queer mirror side. Traffic was light. Cars that now and then passed me on the side I had abandoned to them, honked at me brutally. Cars coming towards me wobbled, swerved, and cried out in fear. Presently I found myself approaching populated places. Passing through a red light was like a sip of forbidden Burgundy when I was a child. Meanwhile complications were arising. I was being followed and escorted. Then in front of me I saw two cars placing themselves in such a manner as to completely block my way. With a graceful movement I turned off the road, and after two or three big bounces, rode up a grassy slope, among surprised cows, and there I came to a gently rocking stop. A kind of thoughtful Hegelian synthesis linking up two dead women.

I was soon to be taken out of the car (Hi, Melmoth, thanks a lot, old fellow)—and was, indeed, looking forward to surrender myself to many hands, without doing anything to co-operate, while they moved and carried me, relaxed, comfortable, surrendering myself lazily, like a patient, and deriving an eerie enjoyment from my limpness and the absolutely reliable support given me by the police and the ambulance people. And while waiting for them to run up to me on the high slope, I evoked a last mirage of wonder and hopelessness. One day, soon after her disappearance, an attack of abominable nausea forced me to pull up on the ghost of an old mountain road that now accompanied, now traversed a brand new highway, with its population of asters bathing in the detached warmth of a pale-blue afternoon in late summer. After coughing myself inside out, I rested a while on a boulder, and then, thinking the sweet air might do me good, walked a little way toward a low stone parapet on the precipice side of the highway. Small grasshoppers spurted out of the withered roadside weeds. A very light cloud was opening its arms and moving toward a slightly more substantial one belonging to another, more sluggish heavenlogged system. As I approached the friendly abyss, I grew aware of a melodious unity of sounds rising like vapour from a small mining town that lay at my feet, in a fold in the valley. One could make out the geometry of the streets between blocks of red and grey roofs, and green puffs of trees, and a serpentine stream, and the rich, ore-like glitter of the city dump, and beyond the town, roads criss-crossing the crazy quilt of dark and pale fields, and behind it all, great timbered mountains. But even brighter than those quietly rejoicing colours—for there are colours and shades that seem to enjoy themselves in good company—both brighter and dreamier to the ear than they were to the eye, was that vapoury vibration of accumulated sounds that never ceased for a moment, as it rose to the lip of granite where I stood wiping my foul mouth. And soon I realised that all these sounds were of one nature, that no other sounds but these came from the transparent town, with the women at home and the men away. Reader! What I heard was but the melody of children at play, nothing but that, and so limpid was the air that within this vapour of blended voices, majestic and minute, remote and magically near, frank and divinely enigmatic—one could hear them now and then, as if released, an almost articulate burst of vivid laughter, or the crack of a bat or the clatter of a toy wagon, but it was all really too far for the eye to distinguish any movement in the lightly etched streets. I stood listening to that musical vibration from my lofty slope, to those flashes of separate cries with a kind of demure murmur for background, and then I knew that the hopelessly poignant thing was not Lolita's absence from my side, but the absence of her voice from that concord.

From *Lolita* by Vladimir Nabokov, 1955

Victims of jealousy seek the ultimate revenge. Here murder depends on the outcome of a curious toss-up.

It was a common, horribly common, act of bloodshed—the murder of a woman in farm-service, by a man of the same employment who was jealous of her. He had been convicted on no extraordinary evidence. He had made his confession, when he knew there was no hope for him, like other criminals of his class; and the newspaper had printed it at the end of the article, in these terms:

> I kept company with the deceased for a year or thereabouts. I said I would marry her when I had money enough. She said I had money enough now. We had a quarrel. She refused to walk out with me any more; she wouldn't draw me my beer; she took up with my fellow-servant, David Crouch. She laughed at me. She turned me out of the washhouse and the rest of them saw her turn me out. I was not easy in

[46]

my mind. I went and sat on the gate—the gate in the meadow they call
Pettit's Piece. I thought I would shoot her. I went and fetched my gun
and loaded it. I went out into Pettit's Piece again. I was hard put to it, to
make up my mind. I thought I would try my luck—I mean try whether
to kill her or not—by throwing up the spud of the plough into the air. I
said to myself, if it falls flat, I'll spare her; if it falls point in the earth,
I'll kill her. I took a good swing with it, and shied it up. It fell point in
the earth. I went and shot her. It was a bad job, but I did it. I did it, as
they said I did it at the trial. I hope the Lord will have mercy on me. I
wish my mother to have my old clothes. I have no more to say.

From *No Name* by Wilkie Collins, 1862

A rejected lover is revenged on the bride in red . . .

No soft pink or peach scheme for Rose-Marie O'Hara when she
　married:
Since her favourite colour was red, she was determined on a vivid
　red theme—
The bridesmaids were in scarlet lace and satin, armed with bouquets
Of vermilion roses; the friend's 'black taxi' which they borrowed for
　the bridal car
Was crimson lake. Into which they'd dive before the day was out.
　The invitations
Were, of course, red letters. My hands were shaking as I slit the
　envelope
And glimpsed the copperplate. My name. His and hers. All brought
　together
In a florid moment, a dashed-off sketch of what would happen, like
　this fox
I caught once in the corner of my eye, disappearing in a brambly
　thicket, its elongated brush
Hovering for an instant like a brush-stroke;
The kind of random mark that might be retained for just that air
Of neither-here-nor-thereness. Coming in the act of going.

[47]

Some might have swamped the canvas in this red extravaganza, but convention
Was deferred to in her own ensemble: ivory organza, a tiered affair
With ruched bodice and hooped skirts, millefeuilles petticoats, and underneath
The trailing hem, if you could only lift it, red stilettos—
Such pretty shoes for dancing in, I don't think—which were, it seemed,
A bit too tight for comfort. Teetering up the knife edge of the aisle,
Did she even regret this? Whispers ran around her and jostled her dress.
Which she'd discard before the day was out.

Now the soles of the groom's feet are presented to me, hers are hidden
Still. She might have stepped into a muddied pool up to her ankles,
Or they are deep in the lacy avalanche. Thinking of *her cheeks like roses*
Or like blood dropped on snow, I would have climbed the Matterhorn for her,
Stood on my head, or run like a fox before hounds—through the copper beeches,
Glowing, bursting into thickets like the last coal stirred in the fire
Of his red hair. I'd blow and blow and try to stir it up again. Though still
I couldn't quite believe it. Like the wrong-sized foot
Stuck into this glass slipper, she was the glass and he was the foot.
Her own feet, lopped off, waltzed away into the forest.
How could I unravel all those brambles, tangles, nettles, thorns? I pulled
At jagged things and more kept coming up in that erratic spiky hand
Of hers. Billets-doux, excuses, lies. Or a line or two that gave some hope . . .

I'd twist it inside out, this coil that led me on and on, and brings me
    back
To the red bud of his buttonhole, a shower of red confetti.

Or to this scenario of her as Wolf, and me as Little Red Riding Hood
Being gobbled up. *Many's the strawberry grows in the salt sea*, as
    the song
Would have it, *and many's the ship sails in the forest;* it's time for the
    fox
To go to earth. I painted a picture of myself curled up, the brush
Like a knife between my teeth. A few careless dribbles, incarnadine
    upon my wrist.
The newly-weds were found in a wood. His face was pockmarked by
    a fever
Of stilettos. Her belly was unstitched. Tomato ketchup flicked on her
    portrait.
Everything dissolves: the white spirit clouds with rust and cinnabar.

                    'All the Better to See You With' by Ciaran Carson, 1989

*Giovanni and his sister Annabella have been lovers. Now pregnant,
she has betrothed herself to Soranzo, and her brother seeks revenge
on both.*

GIOVANNI: The glory of my deed
        Darken'd the midday sun, made noon as night.
        You came to feast, my lords, with dainty fare;
        I came to feast too, but I digg'd for food
        In a much richer mine than gold or stone
        Of any value balanc'd; 'tis a heart,
        A heart, my lords, in which is mind entomb'd.
        Look well upon't; d'ee know't?
VASQUES: What strange riddle's this?

[49]

GIOVANNI: 'Tis Annabella's heart, 'tis; why d'ee startle:
I vow 'tis hers; this dagger's point plough'd up
Her fruitful womb, and left to me the fame
Of a most glorious executioner.

FLORIO: Why, madman, art thyself?

GIOVANNI: Yes, father, and that times to come may know
How as my fate I honoured my revenge,
List, father, to your ears I will yield up
How much I have deserv'd to be your son.

FLORIO: What is't thou say'st?

GIOVANNI: Nine moons have had their changes,
Since I first throughly view'd and truly lov'd
Your daughter and my sister.

                       How!—Alas,

FLORIO:
My lords, he's a frantic madman!
    Father, no.

GIOVANNI: Father, no.
For nine months' space in secret I enjoy'd
Sweet Annabella's sheets; nine months I liv'd
A happy monarch of her heart and her.
Soranzo, thou know'st this; thy paler cheek
Bears the confounding print of thy disgrace;
For her too fruitful womb too soon bewray'd
The happy passage of our stol'n delights,
And made her mother to a child unborn.

CARDINAL: Incestuous villain!

FLORIO: O, his rage belies him.

GIOVANNI: It does not; 'tis the oracle of truth;
I vow it is so.

SORANZO: I shall burst with fury!
Bring the strumpet forth.

VASQUES: I shall, sir.
    (*Exit Vasques.*)

GIOVANNI: Do, sir—Have you all no faith

To credit yet my triumphs? Here I swear
By all that you call sacred, by the love
I bore my Annabella whilst she liv'd,
These hands have from her bosom ripp'd this heart.
(*Enter Vasques.*)
Is't true or no, sir?
VASQUES: 'Tis most strangely true.

From *'Tis Pity She's a Whore* by John Ford, 1633

*The thief has been hanged for stealing treasures from the church to
buy presents for the girl he loves. His brother means to kill her, yet is
reluctant.*

PART I

'I have a Love I love too well
Where Dunkery frowns on Exon Moor;
I have a Love I love too well,
    To whom, ere she was mine,
"Such is my love for you," I said,
"That you shall have to hood your head
A silken kerchief crimson-red,
    Wove finest of the fine."

'And since this Love, for one mad moon
On Exon Wild by Dunkery Tor,
Since this my Love for one mad moon
    Did clasp me as her king,
I snatched a silk-piece red and rare
From off a stall at Priddy Fair,
For handkerchief to hood her hair
    When we went gallanting.

[51]

'Full soon the four weeks neared their end
Where Dunkery frowns on Exon Moor;
And when the four weeks neared their end,
    And their swift sweets outwore,
I said, "What shall I do to own
Those beauties bright as tulips blown,
And keep you here with me alone
    As mine for evermore?"

'And as she drowsed within my van
On Exon Wild by Dunkery Tor—
And as she drowsed within my van,
    And dawning turned to day,
She heavily raised her sloe-back eyes
And murmured back in softest wise,
"One more thing, and the charms you prize
    Are yours henceforth for aye.

'"And swear I will I'll never go
While Dunkery frowns on Exon Moor
To meet the Cornish Wrestler Joe
    For dance and dallyings.
If you'll to yon cathedral shrine,
And finger from the chest divine
Treasure to buy me ear-drops fine,
    And richly jewelled rings."

'I said: "I am one who has gathered gear
From Marlbury Downs to Dunkery Tor,
Who has gathered gear for many a year
    From mansion, mart and fair;
But at God's house I've stayed my hand,
Hearing within me some command—
Curbed by a law not of the land
    From doing damage there!"

'Whereat she pouts, this Love of mine,
As Dunkery pouts to Exon Moor,
And still she pouts, this Love of mine,
      So cityward I go.
But ere I start to do the thing,
And speed my soul's imperilling
For one who is my ravishing
      And all the joy I know,

'I come to lay this charge on thee—
On Exon Wild by Dunkery Tor—
I come to lay this charge on thee
      With solemn speech and sign:
Should things go ill, and my life pay
For botchery in this rash assay,
You are to take hers likewise—yea,
      The month the law takes mine.

'For should my rival, Wrestler Joe,
Where Dunkery frowns on Exon Moor—
My reckless rival, Wrestler Joe,
      My love's bedwinner be.
My rafted spirit would not rest,
But wander weary and distrest
Throughout the world in wild protest:
      The thought nigh maddens me!'

PART II

Thus did he speak—this brother of mine—
On Exon Wild by Dunkery Tor,
Born at my birth of mother of mine,
    And forthwith went his way
To dare the deed some coming night . . .
I kept the watch with shaking sight,
The moon at moments breaking bright,
    At others glooming gray.

For three full days I heard no sound
Where Dunkery frowns on Exon Moor,
I heard no sound at all around
    Whether his fay prevailed,
Or one more foul the master were.
Till some afoot did tidings bear
How that, for all his practised care,
    He had been caught and jailed.

They had heard a crash when twelve had chimed
By Mendip east of Dunkery Tor,
When twelve had chimed and moonlight climbed;
    They watched, and he was tracked
By arch and aisle and saint and knight
Of sculptured stonework sheeted white
In the cathedral's ghostly light,
    And captured in the act.

Yes; for this Love he loved too well
Where Dunkery sights the Severn shore,
All for this Love he loved too well
    He burst the holy bars,
Seized golden vessels from the chest
To buy her ornaments of the best,
At her ill-witchery's request
    And lure of eyes like stars . . .

When blustering March confused the sky
In Toneborough Town by Exon Moor,
When blustering March confused the sky
    They stretched him; and he died.
Down in the crowd where I, to see
The end of him, stood silently,
With a set face he lipped to me—
    'Remember.' 'Ay!' I cried.

By night and day I shadowed her
From Toneborough Deane to Dunkery Tor,
I shadowed her asleep, astir,
    And yet I could not bear—
Till Wrestler Joe anon began
To figure as her chosen man,
And took her to his shining van—
    To doom a form so fair!

He made it handsome for her sake—
And Dunkery smiled to Exon Moor—
He made it handsome for her sake,
    Painting it out and in;
And on the door of apple green
A bright brass knocker soon was seen,
And window-curtains white and clean
    For her to sit within.

And all could see she clave to him
As cleaves a cloud to Dunkery Tor,
Yea, all could see she clave to him,
    And every day I said,
'A pity it seems to part those two
That hourly grow to love more and true:
Yet she's the wanton woman who
    Sent one to swing till dead!'

That blew to blazing all my hate,
While Dunkery frowned on Exon Moor,
And when the river swelled, her fate
   Came to her pitilessly . . .
I dogged her, crying: 'Across that plank
They use as bridge to reach yon bank
A coat and hat lie limp and dank;
   Your goodman's can they be?'

She paled, and went, I close behind—
And Exon frowned to Dunkery Tor,
She went, and I came up behind
   And tipped the plank that bore
Her, fleetly flitting across to eye
What such might bode. She slid awry;
And from the current came a cry,
   A gurgle; and no more.

How that befell no mortal knew
From Marlbury Downs to Exon Moor;
No mortal knew that deed undue
   But he who schemed the crime,
Which night still covers . . . But in dream
Those ropes of hair upon the stream
He sees, and he will hear that scream
   Until his judgment-time.

'The Sacrilege' by Thomas Hardy, 1914

Shortly to be tried for the murder of her lover, Leslie finally tells the whole truth to her lawyer.

LESLIE: I sent for him. I told him I must see him. You've read the letter. I was mad to write it. I didn't know what I was doing. I didn't care. I hadn't seen him for ten days. It was a lifetime. And when last we'd parted he held me in his arms and kissed me, and told me not to worry. And he went straight from my arms to hers.

JOYCE: He was a rotter. He always was.

LESLIE: That letter. We'd always been so careful. He always tore up any word I wrote to him the moment he'd read it. How was I to know he'd leave that one?

JOYCE: That doesn't matter now.

LESLIE: He came and I told him I knew about the Chinawoman. He denied it. He said it was only scandal. I was beside myself. I don't know what I said to him. Oh, I hated him then. I hated him because he'd made me despise myself. I tore him limb from limb. I said everything I could to wound him. I insulted him. I could have spat in his face. And at last he turned on me. He told me he was sick and tired of me and never wanted to see me again. He said I bored him to death. And then he acknowledged that it was true about the Chinawoman. He said he'd known her for years, and she was the only woman who really meant anything to him, and the rest was just pastime. And he said he was glad I knew, and now, at last, I'd leave him alone. He said things to me that I thought it impossible a man could ever say to a woman. He couldn't have been more vile if I'd been a harlot on the streets. And then I don't know what happened; I was beside myself; I seized the revolver and fired. He gave a cry and I saw I'd hit him. He staggered and rushed for the verandah. I ran after him and fired again. He fell, and then I stood over him and I fired and fired till there were no more cartridges.

From *The Letter* by W. Somerset Maugham, 1952

'Nay! I'm no coward,' he replied, 'and I'm true to th' backbone. What I would like, and what I would do, would be to fight the masters. There's one among yo called me a coward. Well! every man has a right to his own opinion; but since I've thought on th' matter to-day, I've thought we han all on 'us been more like cowards in attacking the poor like ourselves; them as has none to help, but mun choose between vitriol and starvation. I say we're more cowardly in doing that than in leaving them alone. No! what I would do is this. Have at the masters!' Again he shouted, 'Have at the masters!' He spoke lower; all listened with hushed breath:

'It's the masters as has wrought this woe; it's the masters as should pay for it. Him as called me coward just now, may try if I am one or not. Set me to serve out the masters, and see if there's ought I'll stick at.'

'It would give th' masters a bit on a fright if one on them were beaten within an inch of his life,' said one.

'Ay! or beaten till no life were left in him,' growled another.

And so with words, or looks that told more than words, they built up a deadly plan. Deeper and darker grew the import of their speeches, as they stood hoarsely muttering their meaning out, and glaring, with eyes that told the terror their own thoughts were to them, upon their neighbours. Their clenched fists, their set teeth, their livid looks, all told the suffering their minds were voluntarily undergoing in the contemplation of crime, and in familiarising themselves with its details.

Then came one of those fierce terrible oaths which bind members of Trades' Unions to any given purpose. Then, under the flaring gaslight, they met together to consult further. With the distrust of guilt, each was suspicious of his neighbour; each dreaded the treachery of another. A number of pieces of paper (the identical letter on which the caricature had been drawn that very morning) were torn up, and *one was marked.* Then all were folded up again, looking exactly alike. They were shuffled together in a hat. The gas was extinguished;

each drew out a paper. The gas was re-lighted. Then each went as far as he could from his fellows, and examined the paper he had drawn without saying a word, and with a countenance as stony and immovable as he could make it.

Then, still rigidly silent, they each took up their hats and went every one his own way.

He who had drawn the marked paper had drawn the lot of the assassin! and he had sworn to act accordingly to his drawing! But no one save God and his own conscience knew who was the appointed murderer.

From *Mary Barton* by Elizabeth Gaskell, 1848

An Uncle's Advice

Yet he, whose trident swayed the waters
Mourned with a father's tears for his dear son,
That son whose features turned into a swan's.
Nor had his hatred of Achilles dwindled;
And as the days went on it grew to madness.
The Trojan War was nearly ten years stalled,
When Neptune spoke to the rough-haired Apollo
(The deity of Asiatic nations)
To say, 'O darling nephew of my heart,
Best of my nephews and my brother's sons,
Who joined me as we built the walls of Troy
(A labour that is now too soon undone),
What of Troy fallen with many thousand dead?
No tears for them who held the falling town?
Even now I have a glimpse of Hector dead,
His body circling streets of his Pergama,
The suburb where he lived. And yet Achilles
More heartless, violent than war, lives on,
He who undoes all that we hope to do.

If he would step within six feet of me,
I'd show him how a trident gets to work
And has three points to every thrust in hand.
Yet it's beyond my powers to face that hero;
It should be yours to cut him short, to take him
The quick way swifter than his eye can catch it,
The invisible arrow of death through soundless air.'
The Apollo nodded yes; it was his pleasure
To join his uncle's wishes to his own,
And floating in the cloud he draped around him
He dropped to earth among the Trojan fighters.
There he saw Paris taking careless aim
At any Greek who happened to advance.
Apollo introduced himself to Paris,
And said, 'Why waste your skill, your priceless arrows
On anyone you see? Think of your brothers,
And make short work of treacherous Achilles.'
At this he showed the way where the Greek hero
Ploughed through a dozen Trojans with his spear;
He guided Paris' bow in that direction,
Then drew the arrow with his fatal hand.
At last—it was the first breath of true pleasure
Old Priam knew since Hector fell to death.
Then great Achilles who outfought the bravest,
Had fallen prey to one whose best performance,
Timid at best, was stealing wives of Greeks!

From *Metamorphoses* by Ovid, translated from the Latin by
Horace Gregory, 1958

Rejected by Jokanaan, Salome demands of her uncle and stepfather that he honour his oath to give her whatever she asks of him. She will not be satisfied with substitutes.

HEROD: . . . Salome, you know my white peacocks, my beautiful white peacocks that walk in the garden between the myrtles and the tall cypress trees. Their beaks are gilded with gold, and the grains that they eat are gilded with gold also, and their feet are stained with purple. When they cry out the rain comes, and the moon shows herself in the heavens when they spread their tails. Two by two they walk between the cypress trees and the black myrtles, and each has a slave to tend it. Sometimes they fly across the trees, and anon they crouch in the grass, and round the lake. There are not in all the world birds so wonderful. There is no king in all the world who possesses such wonderful birds. I am sure that Caesar himself has no birds so fair as my birds. I will give you fifty of my peacocks. They will follow you whithersoever you go, and in the midst of them you will be like the moon in the midst of a great white cloud . . . I will give them all to you. I have but a hundred, and in the whole world there is no king who has peacocks like unto my peacocks. But I will give them all to you. Only you must loose me from my oath, and must not ask of me that which you have asked of me.

(*He empties the cup of wine.*)

SALOME: Give me the head of Jokanaan.

HERODIAS: Well said, my daughter! As for you, you are ridiculous with your peacocks.

HEROD: Be silent! you cry out always; you cry out like a beast of prey. You must not. Your voice wearies me. Be silent, I say . . . Salome, think of what you are doing. This man comes perchance from God. He is a holy man. The finger of God has touched him. God has put into his mouth terrible words. In the palace as in the desert God is always with him . . . At least it is possible. One does not know. It is possible that God is for him and with him. Furthermore, if he died some misfortune might happen to me. In any case, he said that the day he dies a misfortune will happen to someone. That could only be to me. Remember, I slipped in blood when I entered. Also, I heard a beating of wings in the air, a beating of mighty wings. These are very evil omens, and there were others. I am sure there were others though I did not see them. Well, Salome, you do not wish a misfortune to happen to me? You do not wish that. Listen to me, then.

SALOME: Give me the head of Jokanaan.

HEROD: Ah! You are not listening to me. Be calm. I—I am calm. I am quite calm. Listen. I have jewels hidden in this place—jewels that your mother even has never seen; jewels that are marvellous. I have a collar of pearls, set in four rows. They are like unto moons chained with rays of silver. They are like fifty moons caught in a golden net. On the ivory of her breast a queen has worn it. Thou shalt be fair as a queen when thou wearest it. I have amethysts of two kinds, one that is black like wine, and one which is red like wine which has been coloured with water. I have topazes, yellow as are the eyes of tigers, and topazes that are pink as the eyes of a wood-pigeon, and green topazes that are as the eyes of cats. I have opals that burn always, with an ice-like flame, opals that make sad men's minds and are fearful of the shadows. I have onyxes like the eyeballs of a dead woman. I have moonstones that change when the moon changes, and are wan when they see the sun. I have sapphires big like eggs, and as blue as blue flowers. The sea wanders within them and the moon comes never to trouble the blue of their waves. I have chrysolites and beryls and chryso-prases and rubies. I have sardonyx and hyacinth stones, and stones of chalcedony, and I will give them all to you, all, and other things will I add to them. The King of the Indies has but even now sent me four fans fashioned from the feathers of par-rots, and the King of Numidia a garment of ostrich feathers. I have a crystal, into which it is not lawful for a woman to look, nor may young men behold it until they have been beaten with rods. In a coffer of nacre I have three wondrous turquoises. He who wears them on his forehead can imagine things which are not, and he who carries them in his hand can make women sterile. These are great treasures above all price. They are treasures without price. But this is not all. In an ebony coffer I have two cups of amber, that are like apples of gold. If an enemy pour poison into these cups, they become like apples of silver. In a coffer incrusted with amber I have sandals incrusted with glass. I have mantles that have been brought from the land of the Seres, and bracelets decked about with carbuncles and with jade that come from the city of Euphrates . . . What desirest thou more than this, Salome? Tell me the thing that thou desirest, and I will give it thee. All that thou askest I will give thee, save one thing. I will give thee all that is mine, save one life. I will give thee the mantle of the high priest. I will give thee the veil of the sanctuary.

THE JEWS: Oh! oh!

SALOME: Give me the head of Jokanaan.

HEROD (*sinking back in his seat*): Let her be given what she asks! Of a truth she is her mother's child!

From *Salome* by Oscar Wilde, 1894

Hassan has 'done the state some service', been befriended by the Caliph and rewarded with the gift of a house. But when he intercedes for the lives of 'the King of the Beggars' and his lover he goes too far.

HASSAN (*throwing himself at the CALIPH's feet*): O Master of the World, have mercy on Pervaneh and Rafi!

CALIPH: What—those two? Let them have mercy on themselves. They have chosen death, as I am told. The woman has paid me the compliment of preferring torture with her Rafi to marriage with myself. They have spent a pleasant day together: exquisite food

[63]

was placed before them, and the surveillance was discreet. They will now pass a less pleasant evening.

HASSAN: Let not the woman be tortured: have mercy on the woman!

CALIPH: Rise, you fantastic suppliant. Do you dare to ask mercy for these insolent and dangerous folk whose life was in their own hands—who have themselves pulled down the cord of the rat-trap of destruction?

HASSAN: Had you but heard them—had you but watched as I did when they made that awful choice, you would have forgotten expediency, justice, revenge and listened only to the appeal of the anguish of their souls!

CALIPH: I doubt it!

HASSAN: They chose so well! They are so young. So terribly in love. I have not slept, I have not eaten, Master! I take no pleasure in my house and garden. I see blood on the walls, blood on the carpet, blood in the fountain, blood in the sky!

CALIPH: Well, well, I will leave you to these agreeable delusions. Abu Nawas has found me a young Kurdish girl who can dance with one leg round her neck, and knows by heart the song of Alexander. I perceive you will be no fit companion for an evening's sport.

HASSAN: It is only for the torture that I speak: it is only for the woman that I implore. Say but one word: the sun will set so soon.

CALIPH (*angrily*): If thou and Ishak, and the governors of all the provinces were prostrate with supplication before me, I would not spare her one caress of Masrur's black hand.

HASSAN (*springing to his feet and making at the* CALIPH): Hideous tyrant, torturer from Hell!

CALIPH (*coolly as* GUARDS *seize* HASSAN): You surprise me. Since when have confectioners become so tigerish in their deportment?

HASSAN (*terrified*): What have I said? What have I done?

CALIPH: There speaks the old confectioner again.

HASSAN: I am not ashamed to be a confectioner, but I am ashamed to be a coward.

CALIPH: Do not despair, good Hassan. You would not take my warning: you have left the Garden of Art for the Palace of Action: you have troubled your head with the tyranny of princes, and the wind of complication is blowing through your shirt. You will forfeit your house and be banished from the Garden, for you are not fit to be the friend of kings. But for the rest, since you did me great service the other night, go in peace, and all the confectionery of the Palace shall be ordered at your shop.

HASSAN: Master, for this mercy I thank you humbly.

CALIPH: For nothing—for nothing! I make allowance for the purple thread of madness woven in the camel-cloth of your character. I know your head is affected by a caloric afternoon. Indeed, I sympathise with the interest you have shown as to the fate of Pervaneh and Rafi, and as a mark of favour I offer you a place among the spectators at their execution.

HASSAN: Ah, no, no!—that I could never bear to see!

CALIPH: Moreover, as a special token of my esteem, I will not send you to the execution—I will bring the execution here, and have it held in your honour. You dreamt that your walls were sweating with blood. I will fulfill the prophecy implied and make the dream come true.

HASSAN: I shall never sleep again!

CALIPH (*to* ATTENDANT): Take my ring; go to the postern gate, intercept the procession of Protracted Death, and bid Masrur bring his prisoners to this pavilion and slay them on the carpet he shall find within the walls.

From *Hassan* by James Elroy Flecker, 1922

Frisky has been Saverini's hunting dog, but Saverini is dead, murdered by a rival. The dead man's mother plans the next move in the vendetta.

Still the old woman gave her no food. The animal, by now maddened with hunger, kept up her hoarse barking. Another night passed. At dawn the widow Saverini went to a neighbour's house and begged two trusses of straw. She took some of her late husband's clothes and stuffed them with straw to resemble a human body.

Having fixed a stake in the ground in front of Frisky's kennel, she fastened the dummy to it so that it looked like a man standing there, and made a head out of a roll of old linen.

The dog looked at the straw man in surprise, and stopped howling, in spite of her hunger.

Next the old woman went to the pork-butcher's and bought a long piece of blood-sausage. Returning home, she lit a wood fire in the yard near the kennel and grilled the sausage. Frisky, maddened, leapt about and foamed at the mouth, her eyes fixed on the grilling meat, the smell of which sharpened her appetite.

At last the old woman made this steaming savoury mess into a scarf round the dummy's neck. She tied it there with string, leaving it for some time, so that it soaked well into the straw. This done, she untied the dog.

With one terrific bound the animal leapt at the dummy's throat, and with her paws on the shoulders began to tear at it. She dropped to the ground with some of the meat in her mouth; then she returned to the attack, burying her teeth in the string, and tore out more bits of sausage, dropped once more to the ground, and again attacked with mad fury. She tore the face to pieces and reduced the whole throat to ribbons.

The old woman, motionless and silent, watched the dog with tense excitement. Then she chained her up again, kept her without food for another two days and then repeated the strange performance.

For three months she trained the dog to this kind of fight, making her use her teeth to get her food. Now she no longer chained her up, but set her on the dummy with a gesture.

[66]

She had taught her to go for the figure and tear it to pieces, even when there was no food hidden in the neck. Afterwards she rewarded the animal with the sausage she had grilled for her.

Whenever the dog saw the dummy, she immediately quivered all over, and looked towards her mistress, who cried in a shrill voice, pointing: 'At him!'

From 'A Vendetta' by Guy de Maupassant (1850–93), translated from the French by H. N. P. Sloman

The Vengeance of a Skull

HIPPOLITO: 'Tis part of my allegiance to stand bare
    To the Duke's concubine—and here she comes.
    (*Enter Vindice with the skull of his love dressed up in tires.*)
VINDICE: Madam, his grace will not be absent long.
    Secret? Ne'er doubt us madam; 'twill be worth
    Three velvet gowns to your ladyship. Known?
    Few ladies respect that disgrace, a poor thin shell!
    'Tis the best grace you have to do it well;
    I'll save your hand that labour, I'll unmask you.
    (*He reveals the skull.*)
HIPPOLITO: Why, brother, brother!
VINDICE: Art thou beguiled now? Tut, a lady can
    At such—all hid—beguile a wiser man.
    Have I not fitted the old surfeiter
    With a quaint piece of beauty? Age and bare bone
    Are e'er allied in action; here's an eye
    Able to tempt a great man—to serve God;
    A pretty hanging lip, that has forgot now to dissemble;
    Methinks this mouth should make a swearer tremble,
    A drunkard clasp his teeth and not undo 'em
    To suffer wet damnation to run through 'em.
    Here's a cheek keeps her colour, let the wind go whistle,

Spout, rain, we fear thee not; be hot or cold,
All's one with us. And is not he absurd
Whose fortunes are upon their faces set,
That fear no other God but wind and wet?
HIPPOLITO: Brother, y'ave spoken that right;
   Is this the form that living shone so bright?
VINDICE: The very same—
   And now methinks I could e'en chide myself
   For doting on her beauty, tho' her death
   Shall be revenged after no common action.—
   Does the silk-worm expend her yellow labours
   For thee? For thee does she undo herself?
   Are lordships sold to maintain ladyships
   For the poor benefit of a bewitching minute?
   Why does yon fellow falsify high ways
   And put his life between the judge's lips
   To refine such a thing, keeps horse and men
   To beat their valours for her?
   Surely, we're all mad people, and they
   Whom we think are, are not,—we mistake those;
   'Tis we are mad in sense, they but in clothes.
HIPPOLITO: 'Faith, and in clothes too we,—give us our due.
VINDICE: Does every proud and self-affecting dame
   Camphor her face for this, and grieve her Maker
   In sinful baths of milk,—when many an infant starves
   For her superfluous outside,—and all for this?
   Who now bids twenty pound a night, prepares
   Music, perfumes, and sweetmeats? All are hushed,
   Thou may'st lie chaste now! It were fine, methinks
   To have thee seen at revels, forgetful feasts
   And unclean brothels; sure, 'twould fright the sinner
   And make him a good coward, put a reveller
   Out if his antic amble,
   And cloy an epicure with empty dishes.
   Here might a scornful and ambitious woman

[68]

Look through and through herself; see, ladies with false forms
You deceive men, but cannot deceive worms.—
Now to my tragic business. Look you, brother,
I have not fashioned this only for show
And useless property; no, it shall bear a part
E'en in its own revenge. This very skull
Whose mistress the Duke poisoned with this drug,
The mortal curse of the earth, shall be revenged
In the like strain, and kiss his lips to death.
As much as the dumb thing can, he shall feel:
What fails in poison, we'll supply in steel.
HIPPOLITO: Brother, I do applaud thy constant vengeance,
The quaintness of thy malice,—above thought.
VINDICE: So—'tis laid on: now come, and welcome, Duke . . .

From *The Revenger's Tragedy* by Cyril Tourneur, 1607

Gatsby's body is found floating in his swimming pool. He, who loved only Daisy, has been murdered in error by a mistakenly jealous husband.

Wilson's glazed eyes turned out to the ashheaps, where small grey clouds took on fantastic shapes and scurried here and there in the faint dawn wind.

'I spoke to her,' he muttered, after a long silence. 'I told her she might fool me but she couldn't fool God. I took her to the window'— with an effort he got up and walked to the rear window and leaned with his face pressed against it—'and I said "God knows what you've been doing. You may fool me but you can't fool God!"'

Standing behind him, Michaelis saw with a shock that he was looking at the eyes of Dr T. J. Eckleburg, which had just emerged, pale and enormous, from the dissolving night.

'God sees everything,' repeated Wilson.

'That's an advertisement,' Michaelis assured him. Something made him turn away from the window and look back into the room. But Wilson stood there a long time, his face close to the window pane, nodding into the twilight.

By six o'clock Michaelis was worn out, and grateful for the sound of a car stopping outside. It was one of the watchers of the night before who had promised to come back, so he cooked breakfast for three, which he and the other man ate together. Wilson was quieter now, and Michaelis went home to sleep; when he awoke four hours later and hurried back to the garage, Wilson was gone.

His movements—he was on foot all the time—were afterward traced to Port Roosevelt and then to Gad's Hill, where he bought a sandwich that he didn't eat, and a cup of coffee. He must have been tired and walking slowly, for he didn't reach Gad's Hill until noon. Thus far there was no difficulty in accounting for his time—there were boys who had seen a man 'acting sort of crazy', and motorists at whom he stared oddly from the side of the road. Then for three hours he disappeared from view. The police, on the strength of what he said to Michaelis, that he 'had a way of finding out', supposed that he spent that time going from garage to garage thereabout, inquiring for a yellow car. On the other hand, no garage man who had seen him ever came forward, and perhaps he had an easier, surer way of finding out what he wanted to know. By half-past two he was in West Egg, where he asked someone the way to Gatsby's house. So by that time he knew Gatsby's name.

From *The Great Gatsby* by F. Scott Fitzgerald, 1925

A Gangland Killing

The Dutchman came up to the recumbent customer and applied addi-
tional hot towels in mimicry of the attentive ministrations of a barber,
dripping on them especially about the nostrils a portion from a small
unlabeled bottle he had had the foresight but not the detailed reasoning to borrow from the cathouse madam. And hovering about the chair
and making small administrative sounds until he was satisfied that all
was well, he felt under the sheet, took the piece from the slack fingers,
daintily put it aside, lifted the towels where they draped over the chin,
carefully folded them back from the throat, and choosing an already
opened straight razor from the shelf under the mirror and satisfying
himself that it was impeccably sharpened, he drew it with no hesita-
tion across the exposed neck just below the jawline. And as the
thread-thin lip of blood slowly widened into a smile and the victim
made a small half-questioning movement in his chair, a slight rise of
the shoulders and lift of the knees, more inquisitive than accusatory,
he held him down with his elbow on his mummied mouth and
wrapped layer after layer of wet hot toweling that was to hand in the
chromed steamer behind the chair over his chest and throat and head,
and only a seeping pinkness, the color of a slow and tentative sunset,
suffused the wadding, so that he was able with unhurried insolence to
wipe clean the twelve-inch razor, fold it, and drop it in his breast
pocket next to the comb, and after a glance of vindication to the lobby
as if there was there, watching, an audience of numbers-industry
bankers, controllers, collectors, and runners, rubbed the grip of the
Smith and Wesson with the striped sheet, and placed it back in the victim's hand, and placed the hand back in the lap, and smoothed the
striped sheet over the body, and withdrew through the mirrored door,
which closed on the scene with a click, leaving two barber chairs, two
bodies, and two trickles of blood spattering the tile floor.

'There wasn't nothing grisly about it,' Mr Schultz told me, refer-
ring to the very headline that had caught my attention. 'That was
newspaper bullshit. You never get a break from those guys, it was
as beautiful and professional as could be. Anyway, probably the

knockout drops was what killed the son of a bitch. I mean he moved but so does a chicken after you cut its throat. Chickens run around after they're dead did you know that, kid? I seen that in the country.'

From *Billy Bathgate* by E. L. Doctorow, 1989

The lover's letters told the whole story . . .

At the police station he explained that he was a deceived husband. The police chief remarked:

'Isn't this a little unusual? Ordinarily you kill your wives. They're weaker than their lovers.'

The man was deeply offended.

'No,' he protested, 'I would be utterly incapable of killing my wife. She is all that I have in the world. She is refined, pretty and hard-working. She helps me in the store, she understands bookkeeping, she writes the letters to the wholesalers. She is the only person who knows how to prepare my food; I have a special diet. Why should I want to kill my wife?'

'I see,' said the chief of police. 'So you killed her lover.'

The man shook his head.

'Wrong again. The sergeant—her lover—was transferred to a place far away from here. I discovered the affair only after he had gone. By reading his letters. They tell the whole story. I know one of them by heart, the worst of them . . .'

The police chief did not understand. He said nothing and waited for the husband to continue, which he presently did:

'Those letters! If they were alive I would kill them, one by one. They were shameful to read—almost like a book. I thought of taking an airplane trip. I thought of killing some other sergeant here, so that they would all learn a lesson not to fool around with another man's wife. But I was afraid of the rest of the regiment; you know how these military men stick together. Still, I had to do something. Other-

[72]

wise I would have gone crazy. I couldn't get those letters out of my head. Even on days when none arrived I felt terrible, worse than my wife. I had to put an end to it, didn't I? So today, at last, I did it. I waited till the regular time and, when I saw the wretch appear on the other side of the street, I went into the house, hid behind a door, and lay there for him.'

'The lover?' asked the police chief stupidly.

'No, of course not. I told you I didn't kill her lover. It was those letters. The sergeant sent them—but *he* delivered them. Almost every day, there he was at the door, smiling, with the vile envelope in his hand. I pointed the revolver and fired three times. He didn't say a word; he just fell. No, chief, it wasn't her lover. It was the mailman.'

From 'Metonymy, or The Husband's Revenge' by Rachel de Queíroz, 1967, translated from the Portuguese by William L. Grossman

3

'TO BASK IN THE SUN'

Killers for Gain

Most people, if asked to supply a motive for murder, would sug-gest gain or greed: for possession of money, property or another human being. Gain supplies a concrete motive for killing and therefore something easily understood, if not tolerated.

And it came to pass in an evening-tide, that David arose from off his bed, and walked upon the roof of the king's house: and from the roof he saw a woman washing herself; and the woman was very beautiful to look upon.

And David sent and inquired after the woman. And one said, Is not this Bathsheba, the daughter of Eliam, the wife of Uriah the Hittite?

And David sent messengers, and took her; and she came in unto him, and he lay with her; for she was purified from her uncleanness: and she returned unto her house.

And the woman conceived, and sent and told David, and said, I am with child.

And David sent to Joab, saying, Send me Uriah the Hittite. And Joab sent Uriah to David.

And when Uriah was come unto him, David demanded of him how Joab did, and how the people did, and how the war prospered.

And David said to Uriah, Go down to thy house, and wash thy feet. And Uriah departed out of the king's house, and there followed him a mess of meat from the king.

But Uriah slept at the door of the king's house with all the servants of his lord, and went not down to his house.

And when they had told David, saying, Uriah went not down unto his house, David said unto Uriah, Camest thou not from thy journey? Why then didst thou not go down unto thine house?

And Uriah said unto David, The ark, and Israel, and Judah, abide in tents, and the servants of my lord are encamped in the open fields; shall I then go into my house, to eat and to drink, and to lie with my wife? as thou livest, and as thy soul liveth, I will not do this thing.

And David said to Uriah, Tarry here to day also, and to morrow I will let thee depart. So Uriah abode in Jerusalem that day, and the morrow.

And when David had called him, he did eat and drink before him; and he made him drunk; and at even he went out to lie on his bed with the servants of his lord, but went not down to his house.

And it came to pass in the morning that David wrote a letter to Joab, and sent it by the hand of Uriah.

And he wrote in the letter, saying, Set ye Uriah in the forefront of the hottest battle, and retire ye from him, that he may be smitten and die.

And it came to pass, when Joab observed the city, that he assigned Uriah to a place where he knew that valiant men were.

And the men of the city went out, and fought with Joab: and there fell some of the people of the servants of David; and Uriah the Hittite died also.

Then Joab sent and told David all the things concerning the war:

And charged the messenger, saying, When thou hast made an end of telling the matters of the war unto the king,

And if so be that the king's wrath arise, and he say unto thee, Wherefore approached thee so nigh unto the city when ye did fight? knew ye not that they would shoot from the wall?

Who smote Abimelech the son of Jerrubesheth? did not a woman cast a piece of a millstone upon him from the wall, that he died in Thebez? why went ye nigh the wall? then say thou, Thy servant Uriah the Hittite is dead also.

So the messenger went, and came and showed David all that Joab had sent him for.

And the messenger said unto David, Surely the men prevailed

against us, and came out unto us in the field, and we were upon them even unto the entering of the gate.

And the shooters shot from off the wall upon thy servants; and some of the king's servants be dead, and thy servant Uriah the Hittite is dead also.

Then David said unto the messenger, Thus shalt thou say unto Joab, Let not this thing displease thee, for the sword devoureth one as well as another: make thy battle more strong against the city, and overthrow it: and encourage thou him.

And when the wife of Uriah heard that Uriah her husband was dead, she mourned for her husband.

And when the mourning was past, David sent and fetched her to his house, and she became his wife, and bare him a son. But the thing that David had done displeased the Lord.

From II *Samuel* XI

Laurent's desires are for a lazy life, with nothing to do but await the death of his father. Above all, Camille's death will give him Camille's wife.

All his interests urged him into crime. He reflected that his father, the Jeufosse peasant, was in no hurry to die, and that he might have to stay on in a job for another ten years, eating in coffee-shops and living womanless in a garret. And it was an infuriating thought. On the other hand, with Camille dead he was at once Thérèse's husband, Madame Raquin's heir, had left his job, and was free to bask in the sun. Thereupon he gave himself up to the pleasure of dreaming of this lazy life, with nothing to do but eat and sleep and quietly wait for his father's death. But when reality stood out in the midst of this dream he came up against Camille, and he clenched his fists as if to knock him down.

Laurent desired Thérèse, he wanted her to himself and always at hand. Unless he removed the husband the wife slipped from his grasp. She could not come back; she had said so herself. Of course he might have kidnapped her and taken her off somewhere, but in that case they would die of starvation. No, it was less risky to kill the husband; no scandal would be raised; he would merely be pushing one man out of the way so as to take his place. His brutal peasant logic found this method excellent and natural, and his native prudence, even, recommended the speedy way.

He lay sprawling on his bed, sweating, flat on his stomach with his greasy face buried in the pillow where Thérèse's hair had been. He took the linen between his parched lips and inhaled its faint perfume, and there he remained, breathless and gasping, while bars of fire darted across his closed eyelids. How could he kill Camille? Then, when he could breathe no more, he turned over again in one bound on to his back, and with eyes wide open and the cold air blowing upon his face from the skylight, searched among the stars in the blue-black square of sky for some advice on killing, some plan for murder.

From *Thérèse Raquin* by Émile Zola, 1867, translated from the French
by L. W. Tancock

The inheritance Hermann receives from the Countess he has killed will be a foolproof formula for winning at cards.

Three days after the fatal night, at nine o'clock in the morning, Hermann set out for the Z Monastery, where the funeral service for the deceased Countess was to be performed. Although he did not feel repentant, he could not completely silence the voice of his conscience, which kept telling him, 'You are the old lady's murderer!' Deficient in true faith, he was nevertheless subject to many superstitions. He believed that the dead Countess could exercise an evil influence on his life, and he decided to go to her funeral in order to ask her pardon.

The church was full. Hermann had difficulty pushing his way through the crowd. The coffin lay on a sumptuous catafalque under a velvet canopy. The deceased lay in her coffin with her arms folded over her chest, in a lace cap and white atlas dress. She was surrounded by her domestics and relations: her servants dressed in black caftans with the family's coat of arms on the shoulders and holding candles in their hands, and her family—children, grandchildren, great-grandchildren—dressed in deep mourning. Nobody wept: tears would have been *une affectation*. The Countess was so very old that her death could not have come as a surprise to anyone; her relatives had considered her on the edge of the grave for quite some time. A young bishop gave the funeral sermon. He depicted in simple, moving words the peaceful ascent into heaven of the righteous, whose long years had been a serene, inspiring preparation for a Christian end. 'The angel of death found her,' said the orator, 'waiting for the midnight bridegroom, vigilant in godly meditation.' The service was concluded in an atmosphere of somber propriety. The relatives went first to pay their last respects to the deceased. Then came the numerous guests, filing by in order to take their last bow before her who had so long participated in their frivolous amusements. Then all the domestics followed. Finally came the old housekeeper, a contemporary of the deceased. Two young girls led her by the arms. She was too weak to bow all the way to the ground; she alone shed a few tears as she kissed her mistress's cold hand. After her Hermann, too, decided to go up to the coffin. He bowed to the ground and lay for several minutes on the cold floor strewn with fir branches. At last he rose to his feet, pale as the deceased herself, mounted the steps of the catafalque, and bent over . . . At that moment it seemed to him that the deceased cast a mocking glance at him, screwing up one of her eyes. He moved back hastily, missed his step, and crashed to the ground flat on his back. As he was lifted to his feet, Lizaveta Ivanovna had to be carried out on the porch, unconscious. This incident disturbed for a few minutes the solemnity of the somber rite. A muffled murmur arose among those in attendance, and a gaunt chamberlain—a close relative of the deceased— whispered into the ear of an Englishman standing by him that the young officer was the dead woman's illegitimate son, to which the Englishman responded with a cold 'Oh?'

Hermann was extremely distressed that whole day. Dining at a secluded tavern, he drank too much, which was not his wont, in the hope of calming his inner agitation. But the wine only further inflamed his imagination. Returning home, he threw himself on his bed fully clothed, and fell into a deep sleep.

It was night when he woke up; the moon was shining into his room. He glanced at his watch: it was a quarter to three. Not feeling sleepy any more, he sat on his bed and thought about the old Countess's funeral.

Just then somebody looked in from the street through the window, and immediately went away. Hermann paid no attention. A minute later he could hear the door of the anteroom open. His orderly, thought Hermann, was returning from a nocturnal outing, drunk as usual. But he heard unfamiliar steps: somebody was softly shuffling along in slippers. The door opened, and a woman in a white dress came in. Hermann took her for his old nurse and wondered what could have brought her here at this time of night. But the woman in white glided across the room and suddenly appeared right before him: Hermann recognised the Countess in her!

'I have come to you against my will,' she said to him in a firm voice. 'I have been ordered to grant your request. The trey, the seven, and the ace will win for you in succession, but only under the condition that you play no more than one card within one day, and that afterwards you never play again for the rest of your life. I will forgive you my death under the condition that you marry my ward, Lizaveta Ivanova . . .'

From 'The Queen of Spades' by Alexander Pushkin, 1834,
translated by Paul Debreczeny

Perhaps many would commit murder if it could be done by thought alone and the reward was great.

So she murdered a mandarin; lying in bed there; not any particular mandarin, a vague mandarin, the mandarin most convenient and suitable under all the circumstances. She deliberately wished him dead, on the off-chance of acquiring riches, or, more accurately, because she was short of fourteen and fivepence in order to look perfectly splendid at a ball.

In the morning when she woke up—her husband had already departed to the works—she thought how foolish she had been in the night. She did not feel sorry for having desired the sudden death of a fellow-creature. Not at all. She felt sorry because she was convinced in the cold light of day that the charm would not work.

From 'The Murder of the Mandarin' by Arnold Bennett (1867–1931)

To Gain a Throne

There were several historical precedents for the murder of a deposed monarch or of persons whose existence threatened the security of a reigning king. Every deposed monarch so far—Edward II, Richard II and Henry VI—had been assassinated on the orders of the men who had overthrown and succeeded them. Arthur of Brittany, Thomas of Woodstock, Humphrey of Gloucester and George of Clarence had all posed a threat to the crown at one time or another, and had all been eliminated. Richard III himself had early on learned a lesson in ruthless pragmatism from the deaths of Henry VI and Clarence, and he had excellent reasons for following precedent.

The House of York had a history of employing violence for political ends. Richard's previous acts of tyranny, such as the executions of Hastings and Rivers, prove that he was a ruthless man who did not shirk from using violence as a means to an end. He was no respecter of the law and was undoubtedly capable of cold-blooded murder.

[83]

Nothing we know of his early-life experiences and character is at variance with this conclusion. Given that the victims in this case were two children aged twelve and ten, his own nephews, we may assume that he felt he had no alternative but to get rid of them; he may even have been reluctant to take such a step, but his reasons for doing so were sufficiently compelling for him to risk both his popularity and his future security as king, should the truth ever come to light.

Thus the murder had to be carried out in the strictest secrecy. The King took only a select few, who were unlikely to talk, into his confidence. Afterwards he adopted a policy of 'least said, soonest mended'. Even high-ranking courtiers did not know what had happened. But the disappearance of two royal children, one a former sovereign, raised questions in many people's minds, questions that many must have been too scared to voice. It was only later, when the threat of reprisals had been removed, that people began to ask those questions openly, or to speak of what they knew.

After the murder, Richard III may have remained officially silent on the subject of the Princes, but his behaviour is indicative of a man with a guilty conscience. His personal prayer in his *Book of Hours*, dedicated to St Julian who murdered his parents and then obtained God's forgiveness, perhaps held a special significance for Richard. He also planned to found a chantry at York served by no less than 100 priests who would offer masses for the salvation of his soul; enlisting the prayers of so many priests, unprecedented in England, is a strong indication that Richard felt he had some serious sins to expiate.

Sir Thomas More says he 'heard by credible report by such as were secret with [Richard's] chamberers' that the King 'never had quiet in his mind; he never thought himself sure. He took ill rest at night, lay long waking and musing, sore wearied with care and watch, rather slumbered than slept, troubled with fearful dreams. His restless heart continually tossed and tumbled with the stormy remembrance of his abominable deed.'

From *The Princes in the Tower* by Alison Weir, 1992

A curious murder from The Tales of Hoffmann.

'Cardillac sat down on his working-chair again. He wiped the sweat from his brow. He seemed profoundly shaken by his recollection of the past and to have difficulty in gaining control over himself. Finally, he began: "Wise men have a great deal to say about the strange impressions to which pregnant women are susceptible, about the curious influences which such vivid and involuntary impressions from outside may exercise upon the child. An extraordinary story was told me of my mother. During the first month of pregnancy she watched, with other women, a magnificent court festival at Trianon. She caught sight of a cavalier in Spanish dress with a flashing jewelled necklace, from which she thereafter could not take her eyes. Her whole being became a desire for the sparkling gems, which appeared to her of supernatural worth. Several years earlier, when my mother was not yet married, the same cavalier had made an attempt upon her virtue, but had been rejected with disgust. The cavalier observed my mother's yearning, fiery gaze. He believed that he would be luckier now than he was before. He managed to approach her and even lure her away from her acquaintances to a lonely place. There he took her passionately in his arms; my mother grabbed at the beautiful necklace; but the same instant he fell to the ground, dragging my mother with him. Either because he had suffered a sudden stroke or for some other reason, he was dead. My mother sought in vain to extricate herself from the dead man's rigid arms. With his hollow eyes, whose light had gone out, directed upon her, the dead man tossed this way and that with her upon the ground. Her shrill screams for help finally reached some people passing in the distance, who hurried to her aid and released her from the arms of her horrible lover. The shock made my mother seriously ill. She and I were given up for lost; but she recovered, and the birth was easier than anyone had hoped. But the terror of that frightful moment had struck me. My evil star had risen and shot down sparks that ignited in me a strange and ruinous passion. Even in my earliest childhood, I prized sparkling diamonds and the work of the goldsmith above everything. This was taken for an ordinary childish liking for pretty things. But it proved to be something quite different, for as a boy I stole gold and gems wherever I could lay hands on them. Like the most skilled connoisseur, I instinctively distinguished fake jewellery from genuine. Only the genuine article attracted me, fake gems and rolled gold I ignored. At length my innate urge was forced to yield to my father's savage punishments.

"'But in order to handle gold and precious stones I embraced the goldsmith's profession. I worked with passionate enthusiasm and soon became the leading master in this art. Then there began a period in which my inborn impulse, so long suppressed, forced its way to the surface and grew mightily, eating away everything around it. As soon as I had completed and delivered a piece of jewellery, I lapsed into a state of unrest and despair that robbed me of sleep, health and the will to live. Like a ghost, the person for whom I had worked stood day and night before my eyes, decked out in my jewellery, and a voice whispered in my ear: 'It's yours—it's yours—take it—what use are diamonds to a dead man?' In the end, I began to steal. I had entry into the houses of the great, I quickly made use of every opportunity, no lock resisted my skill, and soon the jewellery I had made was back in my hands. Then even that did not dispel my restlessness. The eerie voice made itself audible again, mocking me and saying: 'Oho, a dead man is wearing your jewellery!' I myself did not know how it came about, but I began to feel unutterable hatred towards those for whom I had made jewellery. Yes, an impulse to murder them began to stir in the depths of my soul...'"

From 'Mademoiselle de Scudéry' by E. T. A. Hoffmann, translated from the German by R. J. Hollingdale, 1982

Major H. R. Armstrong, a solicitor in Hay-on-Wye, seems to have attempted several murders by arsenical poisoning. He succeeded in murdering his wife, having drawn up a will for her to sign in his own favour. He was executed for this crime in 1922.

Armstrong had been questioned regarding the small packet of arsenic he had in his coat pocket when arrested. He had said that he had made up twenty of these little packets of arsenic, with which he could dose the dandelions that were causing him so much trouble. Nineteen of the twenty packets he had used; but there was one left, and this had been inadvertently left behind, and had in some fashion got caught up with some letters in his pocket.

'You made it up into twenty little packets?' Mr Justice Darling said.

'Yes, my lord.'

'And with regard to nineteen of them, you gave separate doses to nineteen dandelions?'

'Yes. I noticed that these dandelions died afterwards.'

'That was very interesting, was it not?' commented the judge.

'It was at the time,' Armstrong replied, 'but it passed from my mind.'

'Do you tell the jury that you absolutely forgot about that white arsenic?'

'I do.'

'And the dandelions?'

'The whole incident had passed from my mind by the time when I was making that statement.'

After a few more questions the judge said: 'When you saw that little packet, and you realised that you had got white arsenic in your pocket, did you realise that it was just a fatal dose of arsenic, not for dandelions only, but for human beings?'

'No, I did not realise that at all,' Armstrong retorted. But his voice was not quite as confident now. 'I only studied chemistry at school,' he explained. 'I realise now that every one of those little packets I made up, if they were the same as the one found in my pocket, every one contained just a fatal dose of arsenic for a human being.'

'If you were simply dosing dandelions,' the judge went on, 'why did you make up that one ounce of arsenic into twenty little packets such as that found in your pocket, wrapped up in paper?'

'Because of the convenience of putting it in the ground.'

'But you did it all in one day?'

'I dosed them.'

'All at the same time?'

'Yes.'

'Why go to the trouble of making up twenty little packets,' the judge insisted, 'one for each dandelion, instead of taking out the ounce you had got, and making a hole, and giving the dandelions something from the ounce?'

'I do not really know,' Armstrong was quite certainly faltering now, as he came to realise the pointed questioning of the judge was extracting information that even the Attorney-general had not been able to extract.

'Why,' said the judge slowly, 'make up twenty little packets, each a fatal dose for a human being and put them in your pocket?'

'At the time,' Armstrong replied, 'it seemed the most convenient way of doing it. I cannot give any other explanation.'

From *Murder Revisited* by John Rowland, 1961

A Poisoned Chalice

MACBETH: If it were done when 'tis done, then 'twere well
   It were done quickly. If th'assassination
   Could trammel up the consequence, and catch,
   With his surcease, success; that but this blow
   Might be the be-all and the end-all—here,
   But here upon this bank and shoal of time,
   We'd jump the life to come. But in these cases
   We still have judgment here; that we but teach
   Bloody instructions, which, being taught, return
   To plague th'inventor: this even-handed justice
   Commends th'ingredience of our poisoned chalice
   To our own lips. He's here in double trust:
   First as I am his kinsman and his subject,
   Strong both against the deed; then, as his host,
   Who should against his murderer shut the door,
   Not bear the knife myself. Besides, this Duncan
   Hath borne his faculties so meek, hath been
   So clear in his great office, that his virtues
   Will plead like angels trumpet-tongued against
   The deep damnation of his taking-off;
   And pity, like a naked newborn babe,
   Striding the blast, or heaven's cherubin horsed,
   Upon the sightless couriers of the air,
   Shall blow the horrid deed in every eye,
   That tears shall drown the wind. I have no spur
   To prick the sides of my intent, but only
   Vaulting ambition, which o'erleaps itself,
   And falls on th'other ...

From *Macbeth* by William Shakespeare, 1606

Chappie went over to the card table where Broderick and Yates played gin when someone else was at the wheel. He pulled the plastic bag from under his waistband, turned it upside down, and let the knife and the ear fall out on the table. The ear was putty-colored now, its severed edge a gummy red and brown where the ooze of blood had clotted.

The little smile on Broderick's face disappeared. He released the wheel and walked over to the table, eyes fixed on it. Del immediately grabbed the wheel and steadied it. He said to Broderick, 'What the hell you looking so surprised at, man? He told you he could do it, didn't he? And bring back all the proof you wanted, didn't he?'

Broderick stood staring at the table. Then he stared at Chapman the same intent way, wiping a hand slowly back and forth over his mouth. Finally he said in a thick voice, 'You really killed somebody? I mean, killed him?'

Chappie nodded at the table. 'You think he just lay there and asked me to cut that off him?'

'But who was he? My God, you couldn't even know who he was!'

'I'm in no rush,' Chappie said. 'I can wait to find out when we see the papers over in Freeport tomorrow. But I'm not waiting till then for the payoff.' He held out his hand and wiggled the fingers invitingly. 'Right now's the time.'

'Payoff ?' said Broderick.

'Man, you said it was your ten dollars to my dime I couldn't do it. So I did it. Now it's payoff time.'

Broderick said in anguish, 'But I swear to God I never meant you to go through with it. I never meant you to. It was just talk, that's all. You knew it was just talk. You must have known it.'

'You told him the layout there,' Del said. 'You told him where to look for somebody he could waste. You were the one scared about the chopper spotting us coming back here. Man, don't you start crawfishing now.'

'Now look,' Broderick said, then stopped short, shaking his head at his own thoughts.

Yates walked over to him fast, caught hold of his wrist. 'Listen to me, Brod. I'm talking to you as your lawyer. You give him any money now, you are really in this up to your neck. And you're not taking them to the Bahamas or anywhere else out of the country. We can make it to Key Largo before dark and they'll haul out right there.'

Chappie shrugged. 'Freeport, Key Largo, whatever makes you happy.' He picked up the knife from the table, opened its blade, held it up, admiring the way the sunlight ran up and down the blade. Then he leveled the knife at Broderick's belly. 'But first I collect everything that's coming to me.'

Broderick looked down at the knife, looked up at Chappie's face. Behind him at the wheel, Del said, 'There's two of us, man,' and Broderick pulled his wrist free of Yates' grip on it, shoved his hand into his hip pocket. He came up with a wad of bills in a big gold clip. He drew a ten-dollar bill from the clip and held it out to Chappie. 'For ten lousy dollars,' he said unbelievingly.

Chappie took the bill, studied it front and back as if making sure it was honest money. Then he slowly tore it in half, held the two halves high and released them to the breeze. They fluttered over the jackstaff at the stern of the *Belinda II* and landed in her wake not far behind the trailing dingy.

'That was the nothing part of the deal,' Chappie said. 'Now how about the real payoff?'

'The real payoff?'

'Mister, you told me that if I pulled it off you'd come right out and say you didn't know what it was all about. You told me you'd look me straight in the eye and say there's just as good men in Nam right now as that chicken company you were with in Korea. Just as good and maybe a lot better. Now say it.'

From *The Payoff* by Stanley Ellin, 1971

Murder is unacceptable even in direst need. A man should perish before he takes another's life.

While Davis sounded his foghorn and the buoy bells clanged softly far away, Empson told us the story of Jeb Cannon.

It was the afternoon of July 22, 1904, and the small herring fleet which operated out of Southwest Harbor stood about two miles off Otter Cliffs when a storm struck, scattering the boats. The boat Cannon was on split wide open and quickly foundered. Jeb Cannon, of Southwest Harbor, James Thomas, of Damariscotta, and Clem Mallory, of Ellsworth, were the only survivors of a crew of ten, having managed to reach a small lifeboat. They had no water and food, but fortunately it rained a great deal and they caught the rain in their shirts and wrung it out into the bailing can. The search for them was widespread but futile.

About a month later Cannon was picked up by a herring boat out of Gloucester. There were large chunks of meat in his boat—the remains of James Thomas. Cannon had been eating him. You could see where he'd been working over him with his knife. The head was gone but there was the name tattooed on the left arm. Cannon was blackened and blistered by the sun. His hair was now grey; it had been brown. His lips were black and his nose looked like a bit of black bone. Oddly enough his hands were green as a crab. He became hysterical on board the herring boat and the men soothed him with rum. The story he gave them was that first Mallory and then Thomas had died of exposure and he had eaten them to stay alive.

He continued to live alone in Southwest Harbor near where the sardine factory now stands. He kept mostly to himself and was not one for much jawing, as he put it. Fourteen years after his shipwreck he caught a fever and, sensing that he was dying, called in his neighbors. He gave them the following account of his shipwreck.

He and Mallory and Thomas had drifted day after day, becoming so weak that they lay in the bottom of the boat, barely stirring, waiting to die. One night, about two weeks after the storm, Cannon had shot

Mallory through the head with the pistol he had managed to salvage from the wreck and which he had hidden.

'Cut him up, we're going to eat,' he had told Thomas.

Thomas had glared at him, muttering something which Cannon could not make out.

'I'll kill you,' said Cannon, and he crawled close to Thomas and pointed the gun at his head.

Thomas spat weakly at him and continued to mutter and to glare.

'No,' Cannon had said. 'I need fresh meat.'

He had cut Mallory up and eaten him for several days. But Mallory went bad and he had to toss him piecemeal overboard. He had slept with his gun in his fist. Three days before being picked up he had shot Thomas.

Empson, finishing his tale, said, 'His neighbors, they went out and left him to die alone. And after he died they wouldn't let him be buried in Southwest. They hauled him out in a dinghy and dropped him over the side.'

From *Great Shipwrecks and Castaways* by Charles Neider, 1952

To gain possession of her store of opium, to which both he and she were addicted, was Dr Mowbray's motive for poisoning his wife.

'He stabbed her,' replied Traill. 'He stabbed her in a strange fashion, when she was far away at the other end of the garden.'

'But he was not there!' cried Catherine. 'He was up in his room.'

'He was not there when he stabbed her,' answered the detective.

'I told Miss Crawford,' said the captain in a low voice, 'that the garden was full of daggers.'

'Yes, of green daggers that grow on trees,' continued Traill. 'You may say if you like that she was killed by a wild creature, tied to the earth but armed.'

His morbid fancy in putting things moved her again in her vague feeling of a garden of green mythological monsters.

'He was committing the crime at the moment when you first came into that garden,' said Traill. 'The crime that he committed with his own hands. You stood in the sunshine and watched him commit it.

'I have told you the deed was done for the drug, but not by the drug. I tell you now that it was done with a syringe, but not a hypodermic syringe. It was being done with that ordinary garden implement he was holding in his hand when you saw him first. But the stuff with which he drenched the green rose trees came out of this green bottle.'

'He poisoned the roses?' asked Catherine almost mechanically.

'Yes,' said the captain, 'he poisoned the roses. And the thorns.'

The girl gazed at him distractedly. Then she said. 'And the knife . . . ?'

'That is soon said,' answered Traill. 'The presence of the knife had nothing to do with it. The absence of the knife had a great deal. The murderer stole it and hid it, partly perhaps with some idea that its loss would look black against the captain, whom I did in fact suspect, as I think you did. But there was a much more practical reason; the same that had made him steal and hide his wife's scissors. You heard his wife say that she always wanted to tear off the roses with her fingers. If there was no instrument to hand, he knew that one fine morning she would. And one fine morning she did.'

From 'The Garden of Smoke' by G. K. Chesterton, 1919

Arguments are advanced in conversation for killing in 'the service of humanity'. Raskolnikov has heard them all before but this time they refer to the specific victim he himself plans to kill ...

'Hear me further. On the other hand, young fresh strength droops and is lost for want of sustenance; this is the case with thousands everywhere! A hundred, a thousand good deeds and enterprises could be carried out and upheld with the money this old woman has bequeathed to a monastery. A dozen families might be saved from hunger, want, ruin, crime, and misery, and all with her money! Kill her, I say, take it from her, and dedicate it to the service of humanity and the general good! What is your opinion? Shall not one little crime be effaced and atoned for by a thousand good deeds? For one useless life a thousand saved from decay and death. One death, and a hundred beings restored to existence! There's calculation for you. What in proportion is the life of this miserable old woman? No more than the life of a flea, a beetle, nay, not even that, for she is pernicious. She preys on others' lives. She lately bit Elizabeth's finger, in a fit of passion, and nearly bit it off!'

'Certainly she does not deserve to live,' observed the officer, 'but nature ...'

'Ah, my friend, nature has to be governed and guided, or we should be drowned in prejudices. Without it there would never be one great man. They say "duty is conscience". Now I have nothing to say against duty and conscience, but let us see, how do we understand them? Let me put another question to you. Listen.'

'Stop a minute. I will give you one.'

'Well?'

'After all you have said and declaimed, tell me—are you going to kill the old woman *yourself* or not?'

'Of course not. I only pointed out the inequality of things. As for the deed ...'

'Well, if you won't, it's my opinion that it would not be just to do so. Come, let's have another game!'

Raskolnikov was in the greatest agitation. Still, there was nothing

[95]

extraordinary in this conversation; it was not the first time he had heard, only in other forms and on other topics, such ideas from the young and hot-headed. But why should he, of all men, happen to over-hear such a conversation and such ideas, when the very same thoughts were being engendered in himself ?—and why precisely *then*, imme-diately on his becoming possessed of them and on leaving the old woman? Strange, indeed, did this coincidence appear to him. This idle conversation was destined to have a fearful influence on his destiny, extending to the most trifling incident and causing him to feel sure he was the instrument of a fixed purpose.

From *Crime and Punishment* by Fyodor Dostoevsky, 1866

4

'FORBIDDEN ACTIONS'

Guilt and Remorse

*F*reud held unprecedented views on crime, on guilt and causation. Murder is not mentioned here, but would surely be included under the umbrella of forbidden acts.

In telling me about their early youth, particularly before puberty, people who have afterwards become very respectable have informed me of forbidden actions which they committed at that time—such as thefts, fraud and even arson. I was in the habit of dismissing these statements with the comment that we are familiar with the weakness of moral inhibitions at that period of life, and I made no attempt to find a place for them in any more significant context. But eventually I was led to make a more thorough study of such incidents by some glaring and more accessible cases in which the misdeeds were committed while the patients were actually under my treatment, and were no longer so youthful. Analytic work then brought the surprising discovery that such deeds were done principally because they were forbidden, and because their execution was accompanied by mental relief for their doer. He was suffering from an oppressive feeling of guilt, of which he did not know the origin, and after he had committed a misdeed this oppression was mitigated. His sense of guilt was at least attached to something.

Paradoxical as it may sound, I must maintain that the sense of guilt was present before the misdeed, that it did not arise from it, but conversely—the misdeed arose from the sense of guilt. These people might justly be described as criminals from a sense of guilt. The pre-existence of the guilty feeling had of course been demonstrated by a whole set of other manifestations and effects.

But scientific work is not satisfied with the establishment of a curious fact. There are two further questions to answer: what is the origin of this obscure sense of guilt before the deed, and is it probable that this kind of causation plays any considerable part in human crime? An examination of the first question held out the promise of bringing us information about the source of mankind's sense of guilt in general. The invariable outcome of analytic work was to show that this obscure sense of guilt derived from the Oedipus complex and was a reaction to the two great criminal intentions of killing the father and having sexual relations with the mother. In comparison with these two, the crimes committed in order to fix the sense of guilt to something came as a relief to the sufferers. We must remember in this connection that parricide and incest with the mother are the two great human crimes, the only which, as such, are pursued and abhorred in primitive communities. And we must remember, too, how close other investigations have brought us to the hypothesis that the conscience of mankind, which now appears as an inherited mental force, was acquired in connection with the Oedipus complex.

In order to answer the second question we must go beyond the scope of psycho-analytic work. With children it is easy to observe that they are often 'naughty' on purpose to provoke punishment, and are quiet and contented after they have been punished. Later analytic investigation can often put us on the track of the guilty feeling which induced them to seek punishment. Among adult criminals we must no doubt except those who commit crimes without any sense of guilt, who have either developed no moral inhibition or who, in their conflict with society, consider themselves justified in their actions. But as regards the majority of other criminals, those for whom punitive measures are really designed, such a motivation for crime might very well be taken into consideration; it might throw light on some obscure points in the psychology of the criminal, and furnish punishment with a new psychological basis.

From 'Some Character-Types Met With in Psychoanalytic Work'
by Sigmund Freud, 1915

Murderers, we are told, are haunted by their crimes, and compe.
the memory of the deed to compulsive acts. Lady Macbeth wal
her sleep, ceaselessly miming the washing of her hands. Kelle
built a rockery over his victim's burial place but, unable to leave i
alone, he must constantly disturb it, demolishing and rebuilding.

For a time he dreamt, but of pleasant happy things. He seemed t
filled with a greater content than he had ever known before, a cor
which did not leave him even when these dreams faded and he fo
himself back in the old one.

This time, however, it was different. He was still digging, but no
a state of frenzy and horror. He dug because something told him it v
his duty to dig, and only by digging could he make reparation. And
was a matter of no surprise to him that Martle stood close by looki
on. Not the Martle he had known, nor a bloody and decaying Martl
but one of grave and noble aspect. And there was a look of unde
standing on his face that nearly made Keller weep.

He went on digging with a sense of companionship such as he ha
never known before. Then suddenly, without warning, the sun blaze
out of the darkness and struck him full in the face. The light wa
unbearable, and with a wild cry he dropped his spade and clapped hi
hands over his eyes. The light went, and a voice spoke to him out o
the darkness.

He opened his eyes on a dim figure standing a yard or two away.

'Hope I didn't frighten you, sir,' said the voice. 'I called you onc
or twice, and then I guessed you were doing this in your sleep.'

'In my sleep,' repeated Keller. 'Yes.'

'And a pretty mess you've made of it,' said the constable with
genial chuckle. 'Lord! to think of you working at it every day an
then pulling it down every night. Shouted at you, I did, but yo
wouldn't wake.'

He turned on the flashlight that had dazzled Keller, and surveye
the ruins. Keller stood by motionless—and waiting.

'Looks like an earthquake,' muttered the constable. He paused, ar
kept the light directed on one spot. Then he stooped down ar

scratched away the earth with his fingers, and tugged. He stood up suddenly and turned the light on Keller, while with the other he fumbled in his pocket. He spoke in a voice cold and official.

'Are you coming quietly?' he asked.

Keller stepped towards him with both hands outstretched.

'I am coming quietly,' he said, in a low voice. 'Thank God!'

From 'His Brother's Keeper' by W. W. Jacobs

Poe's murderer is obsessed with the sound of a dead man's heart beating.

I then smiled gaily, to find the deed so far done. But, for many minutes, the heart beat on with a muffled sound. This, however, did not vex me; it would not be heard through the wall. At length it ceased. The old man was dead. I removed the bed and examined the corpse. Yes, he was stone, stone dead. I placed my hand upon the heart and held it there many minutes. There was no pulsation. He was stone dead. His eye would trouble me no more.

If still you think me mad, you will think so no longer when I describe the wise precautions I took for the concealment of the body. The night waned, and I worked hastily, but in silence. First of all I dismembered the corpse. I cut off the head and the arms and the legs.

I then took up three planks from the flooring of the chamber, and deposited all between the scantlings. I then replaced the boards so cleverly, so cunningly, that no human eye—not even *his*—could have detected anything wrong. There was nothing to wash out—no stain of any kind—no blood-spot whatever. I had been too wary for that. A tub had caught all—ha! ha!

When I had made an end of these labors, it was four o'clock— still dark as midnight. As the bell sounded the hour, there came a knocking at the street door. I went down to open it with a light heart,—for what had I *now* to fear? There entered three men, who introduced themselves, with perfect suavity, as officers of the police. A shriek had

been heard by a neighbor during the night; suspicion of foul play had been aroused; information had been lodged at the police office, and they (the officers) had been deputed to search the premises.

I smiled,—for *what* had I to fear? I bade the gentlemen welcome. The shriek, I said, was my own in a dream. The old man, I mentioned, was absent in the country. I took my visitors all over the house. I bade them search—search *well*. I led them, at length, to *his* chamber. I showed them his treasures, secure, undisturbed. In the enthusiasm of my confidence, I brought chairs into the room, and desired them *here* to rest from their fatigues, while I myself, in the wild audacity of my perfect triumph, placed my own seat upon the very spot beneath which reposed the corpse of the victim.

The officers were satisfied. My *manner* had convinced them. I was singularly at ease. They sat, and while I answered cheerily, they chatted familiar things. But, ere long, I felt myself getting pale and wished them gone. My head ached, and I fancied a ringing in my ears: but still they sat and still chatted. The ringing became more distinct:—it continued and became more distinct: I talked freely to get rid of the feeling: but it continued and gained definiteness—until, at length, I found that the noise was *not* within my ears.

No doubt I grew *very* pale;—but I talked more fluently, and with a heightened voice. Yet the sound increased—and what could I do? It was a *low, dull, quick sound—much such a sound as a watch makes when enveloped in cotton.* I gasped for breath—and yet the officers heard it not. I talked more quickly—more vehemently; but the noise steadily increased. Why *would* they not be gone? I paced the floor to and fro with heavy strides, as if excited to fury by the observation of the men—but the noise steadily increased. Oh God! What *could* I do? I foamed—I raved—I swore! I swung the chair upon which I had been sitting, and grated it upon the boards, but the noise arose over all and continually increased. It grew louder—louder—*louder*! And still the men chatted pleasantly, and smiled. Was it possible they heard not? Almighty God!—no, no! They heard!—they suspected!—they *knew*!—they were making a mockery of my horror!—this I thought, and this I think. But anything was better than this agony! Anything was more tolerable than this derision! I could bear those hypocritical smiles no longer! I felt I must scream or die! and now—again!—hark! louder! louder! louder! *louder!*—

'Villains!' I shrieked, 'dissemble no more! I admit the deed!—tear up the planks! here, here!—it is the beating of his hideous heart!'

From 'The Tell-Tale Heart' by Edgar Allan Poe, 1843

Elizabeth I long hesitated and prevaricated over putting Mary Queen of Scots to death.

Three days later, at her court at Greenwich, Queen Elizabeth at last sent for Davison to bring the warrant for the execution, which for so long had lacked her own signature. Davison discreetly placed the warrant in the middle of a pile of other papers which the queen was due to sign. The ruse—for Elizabeth had made it increasingly clear to her ministers that she must be the subject of a ruse—was successful. It was thus, in the midst of an innocuous conversation on the subject of the weather, that Elizabeth finally signed the warrant, with all her other papers, and having done so threw them idly down on the table. But the queen could not quite bear to let this vexatious yet momentous subject, on which she had expended so much emotion, pass so easily. She asked Davison teasingly if he felt distressed so see her give the famous signature after so long. Davison replied tactfully that he preferred to see the death of a guilty person to that of an innocent one. Elizabeth now instructed Davison to get the Great Seal of England attached to the warrant by the Lord Chancellor and then take it to Walsingham. Her vein of humour was not exhausted: 'I fear the grief thereof will go near to kill him outright,' said Elizabeth happily. She then concluded the subject with a practical direction—the execution was in no circumstances to be held in public, but in the great hall of the castle. Elizabeth then laid it down that she personally was to be told no more on the subject until the execution was successfully completed.

Despite this Pilate-like observation, Elizabeth still did not totally wash her hands of the matter. Mary's fears of a secret death were not altogether groundless. Even before Elizabeth had affixed her signature to the warrant, she had been heard muttering in the hearing of her ministers that the provisions of the Act of Association might make it a positive duty for a loyal subject to kill the Queen of Scots . . . thus ridding the English queen of the responsibility. Her ministers, understanding her intentions only too well, pretended not to grasp her meaning. On 1st of February, however, Elizabeth was more explicit. Having signed the warrant, she murmured wistfully to Davison that if a loyal subject were to save her from embarrassment by dealing the blow, the resentment of France and Scotland might be disarmed. The obvious loyal subjects to assume this helpful role were Paulet and Drury at Fotheringhay. Davison's first reaction was to fear yet another excuse for delaying the execution itself. But against his advice, the queen insisted on the point being made to Paulet: a letter was duly sent to the custodians regretting that they had not 'found out some way to shorten the life of that Queen (Mary) considering the great peril she (Elizabeth) is subject unto hourly, so long as the said Queen shall live'.

Now the issue which Mary had so long dreaded was squarely placed before her jailer: and it is one of the ironies of history that Paulet, the man whom Mary had for so long both disliked and feared, hesitated for an instant, but seized his pen and wrote back to his royal mistress in the most trenchant language refusing the odious commission: 'I am so unhappy to have lived to see this unhappy day,' he replied, 'in which I am required by direction from my most gracious sovereign to do an act which God and the law forbiddeth . . . God forbid that I should make so foul a shipwreck of my conscience, or leave so great a blot on my posterity, to shed blood without law or warrant.' Paradoxically Mary was saved from the private extinction which she dreaded by the action of the Puritan who had done so much to make her last months uncomfortable and humiliating. Elizabeth, on the other hand, by a course of action which did neither her courage, her character nor her reputation any credit, gave Paulet a chance to redeem himself at the bar of history—unimaginative, bigoted, petty tyrant he might be, he was still no assassin. It was left to Elizabeth when his answer was conveyed to her to exclaim furiously over his 'daintiness', the 'niceness' of 'those precise fellows' such as Paulet, who professed great zeal for her safety but would perform nothing.

Elizabeth's Council, experienced in the ways of their mistress, did not wait for Paulet's answer before acting. With the warrant in their possession, it was unanimously decided to set proceedings in hand immediately. Elizabeth's ability to continue to toy with the subject despite her signature was confirmed on 5th February when she told Davison roguishly that she had dreamt the night before she was running him through with a sword for not causing the death of Mary. Her interest in assassination was also not exhausted: she appeared to play with the idea of having Mary smothered by Robert Wingfield, pretending this had been the advice of Archibald Douglas. The Council did not wait to see through the full comedy of such behaviour before acting.

From *Mary Queen of Scots* by Antonia Fraser, 1969

According to an 1829 account in the periodical The Gem, *Admiral Burney, brother of the diarist Fanny Burney, attended a school where Eugene Aram was an usher. Aram used to talk to the boys somewhat in the spirit of this poem, presenting his own true experience of murdering an old man as a dream.*

> 'With breathless speed, like a soul in chase,
>   I took him up and ran;—
> There was no time to dig a grave
>   Before the day began:
> In a lonesome wood, with heaps of leaves,
>   I hid the murder'd man

'And all that day I read in school
But my thought was other where;
As soon as the mid-day task was done,
In secret I was there:
And a mighty wind had swept the leaves,
And still the corse was bare!

'Then down I cast me on my face,
And first began to weep,
For I knew my secret then was one
That earth refused to keep:
Or land or sea, though he should be
Ten thousand fathoms deep.

'So wills the fierce avenging Sprite,
Till blood for blood atones!
Ay, though he's buried in a cave,
And trodden down with stones,
And years have rotted off his flesh,—
The world shall see his bones!

'Oh, God! that horrid, horrid dream
Besets me now awake!
Again—again, with dizzy brain,
The human life I take;
And my red right hand grows raging hot,
Like Cranmer's at the stake.

'And still no peace for the restless clay,
Will wave or mould allow;
The horrid thing pursues my soul,—
It stands before me now!'
The fearful Boy look'd up and saw
Huge drops upon his brow.

That very night, while gentle sleep
The urchin eyelids kiss'd,
Two stern-faced men set out from Lynn,
Through the cold and heavy mist;
And Eugene Aram walk'd between,
With gyves upon his wrist.

From 'The Dream of Eugene Aram' by Thomas Hood (1799–1845)

The Pain of Remorse

I tried to find something else to do, but it was no good, and with leaden steps I returned to the kitchen and sat down slowly at the table and spread out the papers in front of me. There it was, a few paragraphs in one of the mornings, squeezed under a photograph of a bandaged survivor of the bombing sitting up in a hospital bed. In the evening edition there was a bigger story, with a photograph of the boys I had seen playing in the hotel grounds. It was they who had found her. There was a photograph of her, too, gazing out solemn-eyed from a blurred background, it must have been lifted from a group shot of a wedding, or a dance, she was wearing a long, ugly dress with an elaborate collar, and was clutching something, flowers, perhaps, in her hands. Her name was Josephine Bell. There was more inside, a file picture of Behrens and a view of Whitewater House, and an article on the Behrens collection, littered with misspellings and garbled dates. A reporter had been sent down the country to talk to Mrs Brigid Bell, the mother. She was a widow. There was a photograph of her standing awkwardly in front of her cottage, a big, raw-faced woman in an apron and an old cardigan, peering at the camera in a kind of stolid dismay. Her Josie, she said, was a good girl, a decent girl, why would anyone want to kill her. And then suddenly I was back there, I saw her sitting in the mess of her own blood, looking at me, a bleb of pink spittle bursting on her lips. *Mammy* was what she had said, that

[108]

was the word, not Tommy, I've just this moment realised it. *Mammy*, and then: *Love.*

From *The Book of Evidence* by John Banville, 1989

Bill Sykes has beaten his mistress Nancy to death, but he has not rid himself of her.

He went on doggedly; but as he left the town behind him, and plunged into the solitude and darkness of the road, he felt a dread and awe creeping upon him which shook him to the core. Every object before him, substance or shadow, still or moving, took the semblance of some fearful thing; but these fears were nothing compared to the sense that haunted him of that morning's ghastly figure following at his heels. He could trace its shadow in the gloom, supply the smallest item of the outline, and note how stiff and solemn it seemed to stalk along. He could hear its garments rustling in the leaves, and every breath of wind came laden with that last low cry. If he stopped it did the same. If he ran, it followed—not running too: that would have been a relief: but like a corpse endowed with the mere machinery of life, and borne on one slow melancholy wind that never rose or fell.

At times he turned, with desperate determination, resolved to beat this phantom off, though it should look him dead; but the hair rose on his head, and his blood stood still, for it had turned with him and was behind him then. He had kept it before him that morning, but it was behind now—always. He leaned his back against a bank, and felt that it stood above him, visibly out against the cold night-sky. He threw himself upon the road—on his back upon the road. At his head it stood, silent, erect and still—a living grave-stone, with its epitaph in blood.

Let no man talk of murderers escaping justice, and hint that Providence must sleep. There were twenty score of violent deaths in one long minute of that agony of fear.

From *Oliver Twist* by Charles Dickens, 1837

In single combat Rustum has dealt a death blow to a young man. It is only when Sohrab is dying that he learns his adversary's true identity and that this is his son.

'Fear not; as thou hast said, Sohrab, my son,
So shall it be: for I will burn my tents,
And quit the host, and bear thee hence with me,
And carry thee away to Seistan,
And place thee on a bed, and mourn for thee,
With the snow-headed Zal, and all my friends.
And I will lay thee in that lovely earth,
And heap a stately mound above thy bones,
And plant a far-seen pillar over all:
And men shall not forget thee in thy grave.
And I will spare thy host: yea, let them go:
Let them all cross the Oxus back in peace.
What should I do with slaying any more?
For would that all whom I have ever slain
Might be once more alive; my bitterest foes,
And they who were call'd champions in their time,
And through whose death I won that fame I have;
And I were nothing but a common man,
A poor, mean soldier, and without renown,
So thou mightest live too, my Son, my Son!

From 'Sohrab and Rustum' by Matthew Arnold, 1853

His nephew murdered for the money in his pockets and buried in his garden, Mr Marble dreads discovery and the ruin that will ensue.

And the hair bristled on his head, and he experienced a horrible sensation of despair as he gradually realised that two out of every three of the criminals mentioned came to grief through inability to dispose of the body. There was a tale of a woman who had walked for miles through London streets with a body in a perambulator; there was an account of Crippen's life in London with the body of his murdered wife buried in his cellar; but the police laid hold of them all in time. On this damning difficulty the book dwelt with self-righteous gusto. At midnight Mr Marble put the book aside sick with fear. He was safe at present; indeed, he was safe altogether on many accounts. As long as he could see that that flower-bed was undisturbed no one would know that there was any cause for suspicion at all. That nephew of his had vanished into the nowhere that harbours so many of those whose disappearance is chronicled so casually in the papers. There was nothing, absolutely nothing, to connect him, the respectable Mr Marble, with young Medland's annihilation. But once let some fool start investigations, even involuntary ones, in that flower-bed, and the fat would be in the fire. Mr Marble did not know whether identification would be possible at this late date—he made a mental note that he must get another book from the library in which he could look that up—but even if that were impossible there would be unpleasant inquiries, and he would be in trouble for certain. Come what may, either he must maintain complete control over that flower-bed, or else he must make some other adequate arrangements. And from those 'arrangements', whatever they might be, his soul shrank in utter dread. They were certain to be his ruin. There would be some unforeseen mishap, just as there had been to the cart in which that man in the book had tried to carry his victim's remains along Borough High Street. Then he would be found out and then—? Prison and the gallows, said Mr Marble to himself, with the sweat pouring in torrents down his face.

One thing would give him security, and that would be the purchase of his house. That would give him security against disturbance for the rest of his life. Mr Marble did not mind what happened after his death, as long as that death was not accelerated by process of law.

But how could Mr Marble possible purchase his house? He was living beyond his income as it was, he told himself, with a grim recollection of five-pound notes changed in Popular Corner Houses. Yet he must, he must, he must. The blind panic of the earlier months had changed to a reasoned panic now; the one object of Mr Marble's life now was to raise enough money to buy that house . . .

From *Payment Deferred* by C. S. Forester, 1926

His boy apprentices have died from Peter Grimes's violence. As he himself lies dying he speaks of his father's spirit and the ghosts of the dead boys which haunt him.

'I'll tell you all,' he said, 'the very day
When the old man first placed them in my way:
My father's spirit—he who always tried
To give me trouble when he lived and died—
When he was gone he could not be content
To see my days in painful labour spent,
But would appoint his meetings, and he made
Me watch at these, and so neglect my trade.
   'Twas one hot noon, all silent, still, serene,
No living being had I lately seen;
I paddled up and down and dipp'd my net,
But (such his pleasure) I could nothing get,—
A father's pleasure when his toil was done,
To plague and torture thus an only son!
And so I sat and look'd upon the stream,
How it ran on, and felt as if a dream:
But dream it was not: No!—I fix'd my eyes
On the mid stream and saw the spirits rise.
I saw my father on the water stand,

And hold a thin pale boy in either hand;
And there they glided ghastly on the top
Of the salt flood, and never touch'd a drop:
I would have struck them, but they knew th' intent,
And smiled upon the oar, and down they went.
    'Now, from that day, whenever I began
To dip my net, there stood the hard old man—
He and those boys: I humbled me and pray'd
They would be gone; they heeded not, but stay'd:
Nor could I turn, nor would the boat go by,
But, gazing on the spirits, there was I:
They bade me leap to death, but I was loth to die:
And every day, as sure as day arose,
Would these three spirits meet me ere the close;
To hear and mark them daily was my doom,
And "Come" they said, with weak, sad voices, "come".'

From 'Peter Grimes' by George Crabbe, 1810

Imprisoned for many years for a murder he did not commit, Aksenof has found peace through his religious faith. When the chance comes to revenge himself on the real murderer, he does not take it. Makar is ravaged by guilt and confesses.

The next day, when they took the convicts out to work, the soldiers discovered that Makar had been digging in the ground; they began to make a search and found the hole. The warden came and asked everyone, 'Who was digging that hole?'

All denied it. Those who knew did not name Makar, because they were aware that he would be flogged half to death for such an attempt.

Then the warden came to Aksenof and said, 'Old man, you are truthful. Tell me before God who did this.'

Makar was standing near, in great excitement, and did not dare look at Aksenof.

Aksenof's hands and lips trembled, and it was some time before he could speak a word. He said to himself, If I shield him—but why should I forgive him when he has been my ruin? Let him suffer for my sufferings! But shall I tell on him? They will surely flog him. But what difference does it make what I think of him? Will it be any easier for me?

Once more the warden demanded, 'Well, old man, tell me the truth. Who dug the hole?'

Aksenof glanced at Makar, and then said, 'I cannot tell, your Honour. God does not bid me tell. Do with me as you please. I am in your power.'

In spite of the warden's efforts, Aksenof would say nothing more. And so they failed to find who had dug the hole.

On the next night as Aksenof was lying on his bunk, almost asleep, he heard someone come along and sit down at his feet. He peered through the darkness and saw that it was Makar. Aksenof asked, 'What do you wish of me? What are you doing here?'

Makar remained silent.

Aksenof arose and said, 'What do you want? Go away or I will call the guard.'

Makar went up close to Aksenof and said in a whisper, 'Ivan Dmitrievitch, forgive me!'

Aksenof said, 'What have I to forgive you?'

'It was I who killed the merchant and put the knife in your bag. And I was going to kill you, too, but there was a noise in the yard. I thrust the knife in your bag and slipped out of the window.'

Aksenof didn't know what to say. Makar knelt and said, 'Ivan, forgive me, for Christ's sake. I will confess that I killed the merchant—they will pardon you. You will be able to go home.'

Aksenof said, 'It's easy for you to say that, but how could I endure it? Where should I go now? My wife is probably dead, my children have forgotten me. I have nowhere to go.'

Makar did not rise. He beat his head on the ground and said, 'Ivan Dmitrievitch, forgive me! When they flogged me with the knout, it was easier to bear than it is to look at you. And you had pity on me after all this—you did not tell on me. Forgive me, for Christ's sake! Forgive me, though I am a cursed villain!' And the man began to sob.

When Aksenof heard Makar Semyonof sobbing, he himself burst into tears and said, 'God will forgive you. Maybe I am a hundred times worse than you are.'

And suddenly he felt a wonderful peace in his soul. And he ceased to mourn for his home, and had no desire to leave the prison, but only thought of his last hour.

Makar would not listen to Aksenof and confessed his crime.

When they came to let Aksenof go home, he was dead.

From 'The Man of God' by Leo Tolstoy (1828–1910)

William Godwin's novel has been called the first detective story. Falkland, a country squire, has killed Tyrrel and allowed two other men to be hanged for the crime. Suspecting Falkland, Caleb Williams pursues him and in his turn, Falkland relentlessly pursues and persecutes his pursuer. His remorse, however, takes a terrible toll.

The preliminaries I have described were scarcely completed before Mr Falkland entered the room. I remember Collins, when he first communicated to me the particulars of our patron's history, observed that he was totally unlike the man he had once been. I had no means of ascertaining the truth of that observation. But it was strikingly applicable to the spectacle which now presented itself to my eyes, though, when I last beheld this unhappy man, he had been victim to the same passions, a prey to the same undying remorse as now. Misery was at that time inscribed in legible characters upon his countenance. But now he appeared like nothing that had ever been visible in human shape. His visage was haggard, emaciated and fleshless. His complexion was a dun and tarnished red, the colour uniform through every region of the face, and suggested the idea of being burnt and parched by the eternal fire that burned within him. His eyes were red, quick, wandering, full of suspicion and rage. His hair was neglected, ragged and floating. His whole figure was thin, to a degree that suggested the idea rather of a skeleton than a person actually alive. Life seemed hardly to be the capable inhabitant of so woe-begone and ghost-like a figure. The taper of wholesome life was expired; but passion and fierceness and frenzy were able for the present to supply its place.

I was to the utmost degree astonished and shocked at the sight of him.—He sternly commanded my conductors to leave the room.

'Well, sir, I have this day successfully alerted myself to save your life from the gallows. A fortnight ago you did what you were able to bring my life to that ignominious close.

'Were you so stupid and undistinguishing not to know that the preservation of your life was the uniform object of my exertions? Did not I maintain you in prison? Did not I endeavour to prevent your being sent thither? Could you mistake the bigoted and obstinate conduct of Forester, in offering a hundred guineas for your apprehension, for mine?

'I had my eye upon you in all your wanderings. You have taken no material step in all their whole course with which I have not been acquainted. I meditated to do you good. I have spilt no blood but that of Tyrrel: that was in the moment of passion; and it has been the subject of my uninterrupted and hourly remorse. I have connived at no man's fate but that of the Hawkinses; they could no otherwise have been saved, than by my acknowledging myself a murderer. The rest of my life has been spent in acts of benevolence.

'I meditated to do you good. For that reason I was willing to prove you. You pretended to act towards me with consideration and forbearance. If you had persisted in that to the end, I would yet have found a way to reward you. I left you to your own discretion. You might show the important malignity of your own heart; but, in the circumstances in which you were then placed, I knew you could not hurt me. Your forbearance has proved, as I all along suspected, empty and treacherous. You have attempted to blast my reputation. You have sought to disclose the select and eternal secret of my soul. Because you have done that, I will never forgive you. I will remember it to my latest breath. The memory shall survive me, when my existence is no more. Do you think you are out of the reach of my power, because a court of justice has acquitted you?'

While Mr Falkland was speaking a sudden distemper came over his countenance, his whole frame was shaken by an instantaneous convulsion, and he staggered to a chair. In about three minutes he recovered.

'Yes,' said he, 'I am still alive. I shall live for days, and months, and years; the power that made me, of whatever kind it be, can only determine how long. I live the guardian of my reputation. That, and to endure misery such as man never endured, are the only ends to which I live. But, when I am no more, my fame shall still survive. My character shall be revered as spotless and unimpeachable by all posterity, as long as the name of Falkland shall be repeated in the most distant regions of the many-peopled globe.'

From *Caleb Williams* by William Godwin, 1794

5

'TO STOP HER CRYING'

Escaping the Consequences

*A*s a motive for murder, escaping the consequences of rash, foolish or immoral actions, is not unusual. To the desperate, it has sometimes seemed the only way out. Disgrace, humiliation, one's own death or that of someone loved, may otherwise ensue.

Here, Mary Ducton reveals the workings of her mind after her discovery that her husband has sexually assaulted a child.

There is no rehearsal for a murder trial. You have to get it right first time. There are no explanations, only deceptively innocent questions to which the most dangerous response can be the truth. She could only recall one question to her in the witness box from the prosecuting counsel and her reply to that had been fatal.

'And what had you in mind when you went upstairs to the child?'

She supposed that she could have said, 'I wanted to see that she was all right. I wanted to tell her that I was there and that I'd take her home. I wanted to comfort her.' None of the jury would have believed her, but some of them might have wished to believe her.

'I had to stop her crying.'

Childhood is the one prison from which there's no escape, the one sentence from which there's no appeal. We all serve our time. She was eleven when she realised the truth, that her father didn't beat her and her brother because he was drunk; he got drunk because he enjoyed beating them and that was how he found the courage to do it. When he came home at night her brother would begin crying even before they heard his heavy feet on the stairs and she would slide into bed with him trying to stifle the noise in her arms, hearing the lurching feet, her mother's expostulatory whine. She learnt at the age of eleven that there was no hope, only endurance. She endured. But for the rest of her life she couldn't bear to hear a child crying.

Murderers often excuse themselves by claiming that they can't remember exactly what happened. Perhaps it's true. Perhaps the mind mercifully erases what it can't bear to recall. But she could remember so much horror. Why then should this particular moment be a blank? She must have tried to shake the child into silence. She must have lost her temper with this wailing stupid girl who hadn't, after all, been seriously hurt, who surely had been warned that she shouldn't go with strange men, who hadn't even the sense to stop crying and get out of the house and keep quiet. At the trial the pathologist described the post-mortem findings. Death had been by throttling; the neck was bruised with the marks of human hands. They must have been her hands. Who else's could they have been? But she couldn't remember touching the child, nor could she remember the moment when what she was shaking was no longer a child.

After that, memory was like a film rolling on with only a few moments when the picture was lost or not in focus. Her husband was in the kitchen. She saw that there were two cups and the teapot and milk jug on the kitchen table. For one moment she had a ridiculous thought, that he was restoring them with tea. She said:

'I've killed her. We must get rid of the body.'

From *Innocent Blood* by P. D. James, 1980

Harvard in the mid-nineteenth century, the grand rarefied atmos-
phere of Boston academe, was an unlikely setting for murder. But
Professor Webster was deeply in debt to his colleague Dr Parkman
and his only way of escape from exposure and disgrace was to kill his
hated creditor.

After chapel, not in the North End but closer by in Harvard Yard, the
Professor took an early Sunday dinner and made his way in the cold
rain to Boston. Everywhere he went he announced what had taken
place the previous Friday: how Dr Parkman had indeed come to see
him; how he had been paid what was due; how he had departed at
speed and that that was the last the Professor had seen of him; how the
Professor trusted, since Dr Parkman was such a man of his word, that
he had indeed cancelled the mortgage. He said this to Parkman's
nephew Mr Blake at three; to Ephraim Littlefield a few minutes later,
rapping his cane on the ground for emphasis; and he made the same
announcement to the Reverend Francis Parkman at his house.

That family, increasingly desperate and anxious, was expecting
something more than such a report delivered as it was, thought Francis, in so very business-like a manner. John Webster was a friend of so
many years' standing. When his presence had been announced by the
servant, their troubled gloom had momentarily lifted, for he had
always been ready with words of kindness and sympathy. But his
behaviour on this afternoon of all times was so peculiarly hasty that it
verged on discourtesy.

The days petered out towards the holiday. The Professor was busy
with his last classes at the College, but was at home at regular times
for dinner and for tea. He played his flute; the girls sang; he tended to
the garden where the grapevines needed their autumn trimming. The
whole College, on both sides of the Charles River, hummed with stories of the missing person. Yes, he had to tell colleagues and neighbors, he had seen him that Friday; yes, the police had of course
searched the College but had found nothing that might help.

More handbills went up around town. The day before Thanksgiv-
ing the Professor was stopped with the girls at a toll-house on their

way to a party at the Cunninghams' and observed a new notice. He read it aloud to them:

$1000 REWARD

Whereas no satisfactory information has been obtained respecting
DR GEORGE PARKMAN
since the afternoon of Friday last and fears are entertained that he has been murdered, the above Reward will be paid for information which leads to the recovery of his body.

Robert G. Shaw

'Will it be found, Pa?' Catherine asked. 'I'm sure I don't know, my dear,' he replied, 'everything is being done that may be.' At the Cunninghams' some mischievous part asked, 'Do you suppose, Dr Webster, that as the last person to see Dr Parkman you may be under suspicion yourself?'

'Why,' he retorted amiably, 'do you imagine I *look* like a murderer?' Polite laughter rippled round the room.

From *Dead Certainties* by Simon Schama, 1992

No one takes Terry seriously. They don't believe what he says, they don't listen to him. Again and again he has been sent back to his family, from school, from Cambridge, from the remittance man's exile in Ceylon. A woman's fastidious unkindness has tipped him over the edge and he has killed her.

On the hall table were two letters, come by the second post, waiting for Josephine. No one, he thought, ought to read them—he must protect Josephine. He took them up and slipped them into his pocket.

'I say,' called John from the stairs, 'what are you doing with those letters?' John didn't mean to be sharp but they had taken each other unawares. They none of them wanted Terry to *feel* how his movements were sneaking movements; when they met him creeping about by himself, they would either ignore him or say: 'Where are *you* off to?' jocosely and loudly, to hide the fact of their knowing he didn't know. John was Terry's elder brother, but hated to sound like one. But he couldn't help knowing those letters were for Josephine, and Josephine was 'staying in the house'.

'I'm taking them for Josephine.'

'Know where she is?'

'Yes, in the chapel . . . I killed her there.'

But John—hating this business with Terry—had turned away. Terry followed him upstairs, repeating: 'I killed her there, John. John, I've killed Josephine in the chapel.' John hurried ahead, not listening, not turning around. 'Oh, yes,' he called over his shoulder. 'Right you are, take them along.' He disappeared into the smoking-room, banging the door. It had been John's idea that, from the day after Terry's return from Ceylon, the sideboard cupboard in the dining-room should be kept locked up. But he'd never said anything; oh no. What interest could the sideboard cupboard have for a brother of his? he pretended to think.

Oh, yes, thought Terry, you're a fine man with a muscular back, but you couldn't have done what I've done. There had, after all, been Something in Terry. He *was* abler than John (they'd soon know). John had never kissed Josephine.

Terry sat down on the stairs saying: 'Josephine, Josephine!' He sat there gripping a baluster, shaking with exaltation.

From 'Telling' by Elizabeth Bowen, 1981

For twenty years the Israelites have been oppressed by Jabin. Deborah prophesies that Sisera, the captain of his host, will be delivered into the hands of a woman.

Howbeit Sisera fled away on his feet to the tent of Jael the wife of Heber the Kenite; for there was peace between the king of Hazor and the house of Heber the Kenite.

And Jael went out to meet Sisera, and said unto him, Turn in, my lord, turn in to me; fear not. And when he had turned in unto her into the tent, she covered him with a mantle.

And he said unto her, Give me, I pray thee, a little water to drink; for I am thirsty. And she opened a bottle of milk, and gave him to drink and covered him.

Again he said unto her, Stand in the door of the tent, and it shall be, when any man doth come and enquire of thee, and say, Is there any man here? that thou shalt say, No.

Then Jael Heber's wife took a nail of the tent, and took an hammer in her hand, and went softly unto him, and smote the nail into his temples, and fastened it into the ground, for he was fast asleep and weary. So he died.

From *Judges* IV

A group of students have killed a man by chance. Their friend, whom they think suspects, may betray them.

Just for the record, I do not consider myself an evil person (though how like a killer that makes me sound!). Whenever I read about murders in the news I am struck by the dogged, almost touching assurance with which interstate stranglers, needle-happy pediatricians, the depraved and guilty of all descriptions fail to recognize the evil in themselves; feel compelled, even, to assert a kind of spurious decency. 'Basically I am a very good person.' This from the latest serial killer—destined for the chair, they say—who, with incarnadine axe, recently dispatched half a dozen registered nurses in Texas. I have followed his case with interest in the papers.

But while I have never considered myself a very good person, neither can I bring myself to believe that I am a spectacularly bad one. Perhaps it's simply impossible to think of oneself in such a way, our Texan friend being a case in point. What we did was terrible, but still I don't think any of us were bad, exactly; chalk it up to weakness on my part, hubris on Henry's, too much Greek prose composition; whatever you like.

I don't know. I suppose I should have had a better idea of what I was letting myself in for. Still, the first murder—the farmer—seemed to have been so simple, a dropped stone falling to the lake bed with scarcely a ripple. The second one was also easy, at least at first, but I had no inkling how different it would be. What we took for a docile, ordinary weight (gentle plunk, swift rush to the bottom, dark waters closing over it without a trace) was in fact a depth charge, one that exploded quite without warning beneath the glassy surface, and the repercussions of which may not be entirely over, even now.

Toward the end of the sixteenth century, the Italian physicist Galileo Galilei did a variety of experiments on the nature of falling bodies, dropping objects (so they say) from the Tower of Pisa in order to measure the rate of acceleration as they fell. His findings were as follows: That falling bodies acquire speed as they fall. That the farther a body falls, the faster it moves. That the velocity of a falling body equals the acceleration due to gravity multiplied by the time of the fall in seconds. In short, that given the variables in our case, our particular falling body was traveling at a speed greater than thirty-two feet per second when it hit the rocks below.

You see, then, how quick it was. And it is impossible to slow down this film, to examine the individual frames. I see now what I saw then, flashing by with the swift, deceptive ease of an accident: shower of gravel, windmilling arms, a hand that claws at a branch and misses. A barrage of frightened crows explodes from the underbrush, cawing and dark against the sky. Cut to Henry, stepping back from the edge. Then the film flaps up in the projector and the screen goes blank. *Consummatum est.*

If, lying in my bed at night, I find myself unwilling audience to this objectionable little documentary (it goes away when I open my eyes, but always when I close them it resumes tirelessly at the very beginning), I marvel at how detached it is in viewpoint, eccentric in detail, largely devoid of emotional power. In that way it mirrors the remembered experience more closely than one might imagine. Time, and repeated screenings, have endowed the memory with a menace the original did not possess. I watched it all happen quite calmly—without fear, without pity, without anything but a kind of stunned curiosity —so that the impression of the event is burned indelibly upon my optic nerves, but oddly absent from my heart.

What is unthinkable is undoable. That is something that Julian used to say in our Greek class, and while I believe he said it in order to encourage us to be more rigorous in our mental habits, it has a certain perverse bearing on the matter at hand. The idea of murdering Bunny was horrific, impossible; nonetheless we dwelt on it incessantly, convinced ourselves there was no alternative, devised plans which seemed slightly improbable and ridiculous but which actually worked quite well when put to the test . . . I don't know. A month or two before, I would have been appalled at the idea of any murder at all. But that Sunday afternoon, as I actually stood watching one, it seemed the easiest thing in the world. How quickly he fell; how soon it was over.

It was many hours before I was cognizant of what we'd done; days (months? years?) before I began to comprehend the magnitude of it. I suppose we'd simply thought about it too much, talked of it too often, until the scheme ceased to be a thing of the imagination and took on a horrible life of its own . . . Never once, in any immediate sense, did it occur to me that any of this was anything but a game. An air of unreality suffused even the most workaday details, as if we were plotting not the death of a friend but the itinerary of a fabulous trip that I, for one, never quite believed we'd ever really take.

From *The Secret History* by Donna Tartt, 1992

*To keep himself from murdering real women, Arthur Johnson stran-
gles a shop window dummy.*

His white lady had attenuated limbs and was as tall as he. Auntie
Gracie's dress came above her knees. She had yellow nylon hair that
curled over her cheekbones. He put the shoes on her feet and hooked
the handbag over her arm. In order to see what he was doing, he had
put a hundred-watt bulb in the light socket. But another of those
impulses led him to take it out. By the light of the torch she looked
real, the cellar room with its raw brick walls an alley in the hinterland
of city streets. It was sacrilege to dress her in Auntie Gracie's clothes,
and yet that very sacrilege had an indefinable rightness about it, was
a spur . . .

He had strangled her before he knew what he was doing. With his
bare hands on her cold smooth throat. The release had been almost as
good as the real thing. He set her up against the wall once more,
dusted her beautiful white face. You do not have to hide or fear or
sweat for such a killing; the law permits you to kill anything not made
of flesh and blood . . . He left her and came out into the yard. The
room that was now Room 2 had been untenanted then as had the
whole house but for his flat. And when a tenant came he had been, as
had his successor, on night work that took him out five evenings a
week at six. But before that Arthur had decided. She should save him,
she should be—as those who would like to get hold of him would call
it—his therapy. The women who waited in the dark streets, asking for
trouble, he cared nothing for them, their pain, their terror. He cared,
though, for his own fate. To defy it, he would kill a thousand women
in her person, she should be his salvation . . .

From *A Demon in My View* by Ruth Rendell, 1976

Raskolnikov, who has murdered the old pawnbroker and her sister, would endure any horrors rather than die.

'Where was it?' said he to himself. 'Where was it that I read of a condemned man who, at the hour of death, says or thinks that if the alternative were offered him of existing somewhere, on a height or rock or some narrow elevation, where only his two feet could stand, and round about him were placed an ocean, perpetual gloom, perpetual solitude, perpetual storm, to remain there standing on a yard of surface for a lifetime, a thousand years, eternity!—rather would he live thus than die at once? Only live, live, live!—no matter how, only live! How true is this? Oh, Lord, how true! Oh, miserable race of men!—and miserable he, too, who on this account calls himself miserable!' he added, after a pause.

From *Crime and Punishment* by Fyodor Dostoevsky, 1866

For some, escape from an unacceptable marriage presents few difficulties. The Duke is a widower now and plans to marry for the second time.

That's my last duchess painted on the wall,
Looking as if she were alive; I call
That piece a wonder, now: Fra Pandolf 's hands
Worked busily a day, and there she stands.
Will't please you sit and look at her? I said
'Fra Pandolf ' by design, for never read
Strangers like you that pictured countenance,
The depth and passion of its earnest glance,
But to myself they turned (since none puts by
The curtain I have drawn for you, but I)
And seemed as they would ask me, if they durst,
How such a glance came there: so, not the first
Are you to turn and ask thus. Sir, 'twas not

Her husband's presence only, called that spot
Of joy into the Duchess' cheek: perhaps
Fra Pandolf chanced to say 'Her mantle laps
Over my lady's wrist too much,' or 'Paint
Must never hope to reproduce the faint
Half-flush that dies along her throat;' such stuff
Was courtesy, she thought, and cause enough
For calling up that spot of joy. She had
A heart . . . how shall I say? . . . too soon made glad,
Too easily impressed; she liked whate'er
She looked on, and her looks went everywhere.
Sir, 'twas all one! My favour at her breast,
The dropping of the daylight in the West,
The bough of cherries some officious fool
Broke in the orchard for her, the white mule
She rode with round the terrace—all and each
Would draw from her alike the approving speech,
Or blush, at least. She thanked men,—good; but thanked
Somehow . . . I know not how . . . as if she ranked
My gift of a nine-hundred-years-old name
With anybody's gift. Who'd stoop to blame
This sort of trifling? Even had you skill
In speech—(which I have not)—to make your will
Quite clear to such an one, and say 'Just this
Or that in you disgusts me; here you miss,
Or there exceed the mark'—and if she let
Herself be lessoned so, nor plainly set
Her wits to yours, forsooth, and made excuse,
—E'en then would be some stooping, and I chuse
Never to stoop. Oh, Sir, she smiled, no doubt,
Whene'er I passed her; but who passed without
Much the same smile? This grew; I gave commands;
Then all smiles stopped together. There she stands
As if alive. Will't please you rise? We'll meet
The company below, then. I repeat,

The Count your Master's known munificence
Is ample warrant that no just pretence
Of mine for dowry will be disallowed;
Though his fair daughter's self, as I avowed
At starting, is my object. Nay, we'll go
Together down, Sir! Notice Neptune, though,
Taming a sea-horse, thought a rarity,
Which Claus of Innsbruck cast in bronze for me.

'My Last Duchess' by Robert Browning, 1842

*The portrait Basil Hallward has painted of Dorian Gray shows the
sitter's own degraded soul. Dorian has no choice but to kill him.*

He could hear nothing but the drip, drip on the threadbare carpet. He
opened the door and went out on the landing. The house was
absolutely quiet. No one was about. For a few seconds he stood bending over the balustrade, and peering down into the black seething well
of darkness. Then he took out the key and returned to the room, lock-
ing himself in as he did so.

The thing was still seated in the chair, straining over the table with
bowed head, and humped back, and long fantastic arms. Had it not
been for the red jagged tear in the neck, and the clotted black pool that
was slowly widening on the table, one would have said that the man
was simply asleep.

How quickly it had all been done! He felt strangely calm, and,
walking over to the window, opened it, and stepped out on to the
balcony. The wind had blown the fog away, and the sky was like a
monstrous peacock's tail, starred with myriads of golden eyes. He
looked down and saw the policeman going his rounds and flashing
the long beam of his lantern on the doors of the silent houses. The
crimson spot of a prowling hansom gleamed at the corner, and then
vanished. A woman in a fluttering shawl was creeping slowly by the
railings, staggering as she went. Now and then she stopped, and

peered back. Once, she began to sing in a hoarse voice. The policeman strolled over and said something to her. She stumbled away,
laughing. A bitter blast swept across the Square. The gas-lamps
flickered, and became blue, and the leafless trees shook their black
iron branches to and fro. He shivered, and went back, closing the
window behind him.

Having reached the door, he turned the key and opened it. He did
not even glance at the murdered man. He felt that the secret of the
whole thing was not to realise the situation. The friend who had
painted the fatal portrait to which all his misery had been due, had
gone out of his life. That was enough.

From *The Picture of Dorian Gray* by Oscar Wilde, 1891

The cook has cast a spell on the captain and he is dying.

The girl watched him for a minute and then slipped out of the cabin.
The moon, nearly full, made a silver pathway over the dark sea. It
shone from an unclouded sky. She looked at it with terror, for she knew
that with its death the man she loved would die. His life was in her
hands. She could save him, she alone could save him, but the enemy
was cunning and she must be cunning too. She felt that someone was
looking at her, and without turning, by the sudden fear that seized her,
knew that from the shadow the burning eyes of the mate were fixed
upon her. She did not know what he could do; if he could read her
thoughts she was defeated already, and with a desperate effort she
emptied her mind of all content. His death alone could save her lover,
and she could bring his death about. She knew that if he could be
brought to look into a calabash in which was water so that a reflection
of him was made, and the reflection were broken by hurtling the water,
he would die as though he had been struck by lightning; for the reflection was his soul.

From 'Honolulu' by W. Somerset Maugham, 1922

[133]

In this passage from Gibbon, the murderers kill a multi-murderer to save their own lives.

But the meanest of the populace were affected with shame and indignation when they beheld their sovereign enter the lists as a gladiator, and glory in a profession which the laws and manners of the Romans had branded with the justest note of infamy. He chose the habit and arms of the *Secutor,* whose combat with the *Retiarius* formed one of the most lively scenes in the bloody sports of the amphitheatre. The *Secutor* was armed with an helmet, sword and buckler; his naked antagonist had only a large net and a trident; with the one he endeavoured to entangle, with the other to dispatch, his enemy. If he missed the first throw he was obliged to fly from the pursuit of the *Secutor,* till he had prepared his net for a second cast. The emperor fought in this character seven hundred and thirty-five several times. These glorious achievements were carefully recorded in the public acts of the empire; and that he might omit no circumstance of infamy, he received from the common fund of gladiators, a stipend so exorbitant, that it became a new and most ignominious tax upon the Roman people. It may be easily supposed that in these engagements the master of the world was always successful: in the amphitheatre his victories were not often sanguinary; but when he exercised his skill in the school of gladiators, or his own palace, his wretched antagonists were often honoured with a mortal wound from the hand of Commodus, and obliged to seal their flattery with their blood . . .

Commodus had now attained the summit of vice and infamy. Amidst the acclamations of a flattering court, he was unable to disguise, from himself, that he had deserved the contempt and hatred of every man of sense and virtue in his empire. His ferocious spirit was irritated by the consciousness of that hatred, by the envy of every kind of merit, by the just apprehension of danger, and by the habit of slaughter, which he contracted in his daily amusements. History has preserved a long list of consular senators sacrificed to his wanton suspicion, which sought out, with peculiar anxiety, those unfortunate persons connected, however remotely, with the family of the Antonines, without sparing even the ministers of his crimes or pleasures. His cruelty proved at last fatal to himself. He had shed with impunity the noblest blood of Rome; he perished as soon as he was dreaded by his own domestics. Marcia his favourite concubine, Eclectus his chamberlain, and Lætus his Prætorian præfect, alarmed by the fate of their companions and predecessors, resolved to prevent the destruction which every hour hung over their heads, either from the mad caprice of the tyrant, or the sudden indignation of the people. Marcia seized the occasion of presenting a draught of wine to her lover, after he had fatigued himself with hunting some wild beasts. Commodus retired to sleep; but whilst he was labouring with the effects of poison and drunkenness, a robust youth, by profession a wrestler, entered his chamber and strangled him without resistance. The body was secretly conveyed out of the palace, before the least suspicion was entertained in the city, or even in the court, of the emperor's death.

From *The Decline and Fall of the Roman Empire* by Edward Gibbon, 1776–88

A doctor dreams of escape from an unhappy marriage for the woman he loves. He castigates himself and half-justifies his actions through an interior dialogue.

– Can a man let the woman he loves be outraged, despoiled, trampled on, before his very eyes?
– Be quiet! She loves someone else. This is his business, not mine.
– You know you love her. Therefore it's your business.
– Be quiet! . . . I'm a doctor. And you want me hugger-mugger to murder an old man who comes to me for help!
– You're a doctor. How many times haven't you uttered that expression: Your duty as a doctor. Well, here it is now: perfectly clear, I think. Your duty as a doctor is to help the person who can and should be helped, and cut away the rotten flesh which is spoiling the healthy. Certainly, there's no glory to be reaped: you can't let anyone know of it or you'll be sitting inside Långholmen or Konradsberg.

Afterwards I recall how a sudden gust of wind blew the curtain against the lamp, how its fringe caught fire and how I instantly stifled the little blue flame in my hand and shut the window. I did these things automatically, almost without being aware of it. The rain lashed the window-pane. The lights burnt on, still and stiff. On one of them was a little fragile grey night-moth.

I sat staring at the stiff flames of the lamps, as if I wasn't there at all. I fancy I sank into a sort of coma. Maybe I slept a while. But suddenly I gave a start, as if from a violent shock, and remembered everything: the question that had to be solved, the decision to be taken, before I could go to rest.

– Well, then, you *don't* want to: *why* don't you want to?

– I'm frightened. First and foremost, frightened of being found out and 'punished'. I don't underestimate your prudence and thoughtfulness on my behalf, and I can quite believe you will arrange everything so that it turns out satisfactorily. I deem it probable. But, even so, the risk is there. Chance . . . One never knows what can happen.

– One has to risk something in this world. You wanted to act. Have you forgotten what you wrote here in your diary not so many weeks ago, before we knew anything of all that has happened since? Position, respectability, future, all these things you were ready to stow aboard the first ship to come by laden with action . . . Have you forgotten that? Shall I turn up the page?

– No, I haven't forgotten. But it wasn't true! I was bragging. I feel different, now I see the ship coming. Surely you can understand I never imagined it could be such a satanic ghost-ship? I was boasting. I tell you. Lying! No one can hear us; I can be honest. My life is empty, wretched, I see no sense in it; yet I cling to it; I like to walk in the sunshine and observe the crowd. I don't want to have something to hide and be frightened of. Leave me in peace!

– Peace, no—you won't have any peace, anyway. Do you want to see the woman you love drowning in a cess-pool, when by one bold swift action I can help her out? Will I have any peace then, can I ever be at peace, if I turn my back on her and go out into the sunshine and look at the crowd? Will that be peace?

– I'm frightened. Not so much that I'll be found out; I've always got my pills and can quit the game if people begin to smell a rat. But I'm scared of myself. What do I know about myself? I'm frightened of getting involved in something that binds and entangles me, never lets me go. What you require of me meets with no obstacle in my views; it's an action of which, in anyone else, I should approve, providing I knew what I know; but it's not my line of country. It conflicts with my inclinations, habits, instincts, everything that's essentially me. I'm not made for such things, I tell you. There are thousands of brisk, capital fellows who will as soon kill a man as a fly. Why can't one of them do it? I'm afraid of having a bad conscience, for that's what you get if you try to shuffle out of your skin. To behave yourself means to know your limitations and I want to behave myself.

Every day people commit with the greatest ease and pleasure actions which fly in the face of their deepest and best-found opinions, and their consciences thrive like little fish in water. But try to act against your own innermost structure, and then you'll hear how your conscience screams! Then you'll hear feline music! You say I've been begging and pleading for an action to commit—it's impossible, it simply isn't true, there must be some misunderstanding. It's unthinkable I ever had so insane a wish—I who am a born looker-on, who want to sit comfortably in my box and see how people on the stage murder each other, while I myself have no business there. I want to stay outside. Leave me in peace!

From *Dr Glas* by Hjalmar Söderberg, 1905, translated from the Swedish by Paul Britten Austin

Gwendolen Grandcourt has wished so passionately for the death of
her husband that it is almost as if she has killed him. She recounts the
tale of an accidental drowning to Daniel Deronda.

'No, no,' said Gwendolen—the dread of his leaving her bringing back
her power of speech. She went on with her low-toned eagerness, 'I
want to tell you what it was that came over me in that boat. I was full
of rage at being obliged to go—full of rage—and I could do nothing
but sit there like a galley-slave. And then we got away—out of the
port—into the deep—and everything was still—and we never looked
at each other, only he spoke to order me—and the very light about me
seemed to hold me a prisoner and force me to sit as I did. It came over
me that when I was a child I used to fancy sailing away into a world
where people were not forced to live with anyone they did not like—I
did not like my father-in-law to come home. And now, I thought, just
the opposite had come to me. I had stept into a boat, and my life was a
sailing and sailing away—gliding on and no help—always into solitude with *him*, away from deliverance. And because I felt more helpless than ever, my thoughts went out over worse things—I longed for
worse things—I had cruel wishes—I fancied impossible ways of—I
did not want to die myself; I was afraid of our being drowned
together. If it had been any use I should have prayed—I should have
prayed that something might befall him. I should have prayed that he
might sink out of my sight and leave me alone. I knew no way of
killing him there, but I did, I did kill him in my thoughts.'

She sank into silence for a minute, submerged by the weight of
memory which no words could represent.

'But yet all the while I felt that I was getting more wicked. And
what had been with me so much, came to me just then—what you
once said—about dreading to increase my wrongdoing and my
remorse—I should hope for nothing then. It was all like a writing of
fire within me. Getting wicked was misery—being shut out for ever
from knowing what you—what better lives were. That had always
been coming back to me in the midst of bad thoughts—it came back
to me then—but yet with a despair—a feeling that it was no use—evil

wishes were too strong. I remember then letting go the tiller and saying "God help me!" But then I was forced to take it again and blotted everything dim, till, in the midst of them—I don't know how it was—he was turning the sail—there was a gust—he was struck—I know nothing—I only know that I saw my wish outside me.'

She began to speak more hurriedly, and in more of a whisper.

'I saw him sink, and my heart gave a leap as if it were going out of me. I think I did not move. I kept my hands tight. It was long enough for me to be glad, and yet to think it was no use—he would come up again. And he *was* come—farther off—the boat had moved. It was all like lightning. "The rope!" he called out in a voice—not his own—I hear it now—and I stooped for the rope—I felt I must—I felt sure he could swim, and he would come back whether or not, and I dreaded him. That was in my mind—he would come back. But he was gone down again, and I had the rope in my hand—no, there he was again—his face above the water—and he cried again—and I held my hand, and my heart said, "Die!"—and he sank; and I felt "It is done—I am wicked, I am lost!"—and I had the rope in my hand—I don't know what I thought—I was leaping away from myself—I would have saved him then. I was leaping from my crime, and there it was—close to me as I fell—there was the dead face, dead, dead. It can never be altered. That was what happened. That was what I did. You know it all. It can never be altered.'

From *Daniel Deronda* by George Eliot, 1876

One woman's object in killing was escape from a violent, abusive and alcoholic husband.

Sara knew that if Malcolm's temper didn't cool there would be violence that night. Alcoholics Anonymous had taught her to leave a situation if it was becoming fraught, so she walked into the kitchen, praying. She knew she had to get him to bed and that she couldn't leave him downstairs. She couldn't sleep knowing that he could either set the house on fire or erupt into a furious rage.

She decided she needed to arm herself just in case, and looked for Malcolm's truncheon in the kitchen, but could not find it in its usual drawer. She expected him to burst in on her at any moment and so, when she couldn't find the truncheon, picked up a knife that was lying on the sideboard. Feeling at least Malcolm's equal she went back into the living room. She wanted to frighten him and by doing so forestall any violence.

Malcolm didn't need any weapon to frighten Sara, just his fist and his tongue. He started to goad her again, calling her a whore and accusing her of being after his money. As far as Sara was aware he had by that time spent everything on drink, but she recognised the paranoia. He was forever telling her that his first two wives had taken him for his money, and when drunk he would accuse her of trying to do the same. There was no foundation for any of this; just as with his sexual jealousy, it was a classic, textbook paranoia.

He told Sara that she wouldn't get him to move, but she asked him again to come to bed; at one point she sat down on the sofa beside him. He taunted her with his inaction, saying, 'Come on, yeah.' She felt he was goading her into striking him as if a bit of him, in his self-destructive stupor, wanted her to lash out at him.

Calmly and deliberately she held the knife over him. One part of her was thinking that if he saw her apparently prepared to use the knife she might shock him just enough for him to stop her and say, 'Enough is enough, I'm sorry.'

From *Sara Thornton, The Story of a Woman Who Killed*
by Jennifer Nadel, 1993

By employing a 'foul villain' to rid her of the man to whom she has been betrothed, Beatrice has become 'a woman dipped in blood'. Her plan rebounds with bizarre consequences.

BEATRICE: Oh I never shall!
    Speak if yet further off, that I may lose
    What has been spoken, and no sound remain on't.
    I would not hear so much offence again
    For such another deed.
DE FLORES: Soft, lady, soft,—
    The last is not yet paid for. Oh, this act
    Has put me into spirit, I was as greedy on't
    As the parched earth of moisture, when the clouds weep.
    Did you not mark, I wrought myself into't
    Nay, sued and kneeled for't; why was all that pains took?
    You see I have thrown contempt upon your gold,
    Not that I want it not, for I do piteously;
    In order I will come unto't, and make use on't,
    But 'twas not held so precious to begin with;
    For I place wealth after the heels of pleasure,
    And were I not resolved in my belief
    That thy virginity were perfect in thee,
    I should but take my recompense with grudging,
    As if I had but half my hopes I agreed for.
BEATRICE: Why, 'tis impossible thou can'st be so wicked,
    Or shelter such a cunning cruelty,
    To make his death the murderer of mine honour?
    Thy language is so bold and vicious,
    I cannot see which way I can forgive it
    With any modesty.
DE FLORES: Push, you forget yourself!
    A woman dipped in blood, and talk of modesty?
BEATRICE: Oh misery of sin! Would I had been bound
    Perpetually unto my living hate
    In that Piracquo, than to hear these words.

Think but upon the distance that creation
Set 'twixt thy blood and mine, and keep thee there.
DE FLORES: Look but into your conscience, read me there,
'Tis a true book, you'll find me there your equal:
Push, fly not to your birth, but settle you
In what the act has made you; y'are no more now.
You must forget your parentage to me:
Y'are the deed's creature; by that name
You lost your first condition; and I challenge you,
As peace and innocency has turned you out,
And made you one with me.
BEATRICE: With thee, foul villain?
DE FLORES: Yes, my fair murd'ress; do you urge me?
Though thou writ'st maid, thou whore in thy affection!
'Twas changed from thy first love, and that's a kind
Of whoredom in thy heart; and he's changed now,
To bring thy second on, thy Alsemero,
Whom—by all sweets that ever darkness tasted—
If I enjoy thee not, thou ne'er enjoy'st;
I'll blast the hopes and joys of marriage,
I'll confess all,—my life I rate at nothing.
BEATRICE: De Flores!
DE FLORES: I shall rest from all lovers' plagues then;
I live in pain now: that shooting eye
Will burn my heart to cinders.
BEATRICE: Oh sir, hear me!
DE FLORES: She that in life and love refuses me,
In death and shame my partner shall she be.
BEATRICE: Stay, hear me once for all; (*Kneeling*.) I make thee master
Of all the wealth I have in gold and jewels:
Let me go poor unto my bed with honour,
And I am rich in all things.
DE FLORES: Let this silence thee:
The wealth of all Valencia shall not buy
My pleasure from me;

[142]

Can you weep fate from its determined purpose?
So soon may you weep me.

BEATRICE: Vengeance begins;
Murder I see is followed by more sins.
Was my creation in the womb so cursed,
It must engender with a viper first?

DE FLORES: Come, rise, and shroud your blushes in my bosom;
(*Raises her.*)
Silence is one of pleasure's best receipts.
Thy peace is wrought for ever in this yielding.
'Las, how the turtle pants! Thou'lt love anon
What thou so fear'st and faint'st to venture on.

From *The Changeling* by Thomas Middleton and William Rowley, 1622

6

'FOR LOVE AND NOT FOR HATE'

Killing from Altruism or Duty

*If taking the life of another can ever be meritorious it may be when
that life is seen as not worth living.*
*Only her death can save the maiden Virginia from Apius' lechery.
Her father tells her what she must do.*

And whan this worthy knyght Virginius,
Thurgh sentence of this justice Apius,
Moste by force his deere doghter yiven
Unto the juge, in lecherie to lyven,
He gooth hym hoom, and sette him in his halle,
And leet anon his deere doghter calle,
And with a face deed as asshen colde,
Upon hir humble face he gan biholde,
With fadres pitee stikynge thurgh his herte,
Al wolde he from his purpos nat converte.

'Doghter,' quod he, 'Virginia, by thy name,
Ther been two weyes, outher deeth or shame,
That thou most suffre; allas, that I was bore!
For nevere thou deservedest wherfore
To dyen with a swerd or with a knyf.
O deere doghter, endere of my lyf,
Which I have fostred up with swich pleasaunce
That thou were nevere out of my remembraunce!
O doghter, which that art my laste wo,
And in my lyf my laste joye also,
O gemme of chastitee, in pacience,
Take thou thy deeth, for this is my sentence.

[147]

For love, and nat for hate, thou most be deed;
My pitous hand moot smyten of thyn heed.
Allas, that evere Apius thee say!
Thus hath he falsly jugged the today' —
And told hire all the cas, as ye bifore
Han herd; nay needeth for to telle it moore.
  'O mercy, deere fader,' quod this mayde,
And with that word she bothe hir armes layde
Aboute his nekke, as she was wont to do.
The teeres bruste out of hir eyen two,
And seyde, 'Goode fader, shal I dye?
Is ther no grace, is ther no remedye?'
  'No, certes, deere doghter myn,' quod he.

From *The Physician's Tale* by Geoffrey Chaucer, fourteenth century

*Similar deaths, or mercy killings, are the fate of the daughters of two
black women, one a slave, the other the descendant of slaves.*

We were black, we were black,
    We had no claim to love and bliss,
What marvel if each went to wrack?
    They wrung my cold hands out of his,
They dragged him—where? I crawled to touch
His blood's mark in the dust . . . not much,
    Ye Pilgrim-souls, though plain as *this*!

Wrong, followed by a deeper wrong!
    Mere grief's too good for such as I:
So the white men brought the shame ere long
    To strangle the sob of my agony.
They would not leave me for my dull
Wet eyes!—it was too merciful
    To let me weep pure tears and die.

I am black, I am black!
  I wore a child upon my breast,
An amulet that hung too slack,
  And, in my unrest, could not rest:
Thus we went moaning, child and mother,
One to another, one to another,
  Until all ended for the best.

For hark! I will tell you low, low,
  I am black, you see,—
And the babe who lay on my bosom so,
  Was far too white, too white for me;
As white as the ladies who scorned to pray
Beside me at church but yesterday,
  Though my tears had washed a place for my knee.

My own, own child! I could not bear
  To look in his face, it was so white;
I covered him up with a kerchief there,
  I covered his face in close and tight:
And he moaned and struggled, as well might be
For the white child wanted his liberty—
  Ha, ha! he wanted the master-right.

He moaned and beat with his head and feet,
  His little feet that never grew;
He struck them out, as it was meet,
  Against my heart to break it through:
I might have sung and made him mild,
But I dared not sing to the white-faced child
  The only song I knew.

From 'The Runaway Slave at Pilgrim's Point' by
Elizabeth Barrett Browning, 1850

The Magical Best Thing

Denver thought she understood the connection between her mother and Beloved: Sethe was trying to make up for the handsaw; Beloved was making her pay for it. But there would never be an end to that, and seeing her mother diminished shamed and infuriated her. Yet she knew Sethe's greatest fear was the same one Denver had in the beginning—that Beloved might leave. That before Sethe could make her understand what it meant—what it took to drag the teeth of that saw under the little chin; to feel the baby blood pump like oil in her hands; to hold her face so her head would stay on; to squeeze her so she could absorb, still, the death spasms that shot through that adored body, plump and sweet with life—Beloved might leave. Leave before Sethe could make her realize that worse than that—far worse—was what Baby Suggs died of, what Ella knew, what Stamp saw and what made Paul D tremble. That anybody white could take your whole self for anything that came to mind. Not just work, kill, or maim you, but dirty you. Dirty you so bad you couldn't like yourself anymore. Dirty you so bad you forgot who you were and couldn't think it up. And though she and others lived through and got over it, she could never let it happen to her own. The best thing she was, was her children. Whites might dirty *her* all right, but not her best thing, her beautiful, magical best thing—the part of her that was clean. No undreamable dreams about whether the headless, feetless torso hanging in the tree was her husband or Paul A; whether the bubbling-hot girls in the colored-school fire set by patriots included her daughter; whether a gang of whites invaded her daughter's private parts, soiled her daughter's thighs and threw her daughter out of the wagon. *She* might have to work the slaughterhouse yard, but not her daughter.

And no one, nobody on this earth, would list her daughter's characteristics on the animal side of the paper. No. Oh no. Maybe Baby Suggs could worry about it, live with the likelihood of it; Sethe had refused—and refused still.

From *Beloved* by Toni Morrison, 1987

Alice is kind and generous, but her tactless do-gooding harms its recipients. Though he sees killing her as the only solution if her family is to be spared pain and misery, her husband first tries to make her change her ways.

'Listen,' he said, 'because I'm going to tell you the truth . . .'

'Don't tell me anything tonight. I'm tired and you're tired . . .'

'I'm going to tell you the truth about yourself, and I'm going to do it now, because it may be too late tomorrow. Alice, you're the salt of the earth. In all the twenty years I've known you, I've never seen you fail once in courage or generosity. You wouldn't tell a lie if you were to gain a million pounds by it. You'd hold your hand in the fire to save a person or a principle you valued. You'd give away your last crust to anyone you felt as kin. I know perfectly well that now you've learnt Madge is hard up you'll cover her with presents, even if it means you have to go without things yourself. And besides that, you've got a kind of touching, childish quality—a kind of—a kind of . . .'

'Jimmy, what's the matter with you? Why, you're almost crying! What's the . . .'

'Well, we'll leave that. The point is that nobody likes having salt rubbed into their wounds, even if it is the salt of the earth.'

He bent over her like a boxer bending at a recumbent adversary to see how his blow had told; but her blunt gaze returned his steadily. 'I'm afraid I'm not clever enough for this,' she said steadily. 'I haven't the vaguest notion of what you're driving at.'

'I'm trying to tell you that you hurt people. You hurt them continually and intolerably. You find out everybody's vulnerable point and you shoot arrows at it, sharp, venomed arrows. They stick, and from time to time you give them a twist.'

'Jimmy . . .'

'I know why you want to talk to Walter. You'll point out to him that he's been sharp to Madge several times lately, and that she's probably a dying woman. That'll harrow him. It'll add remorse to the agony he'll be filled with by the dread of losing her. It'll turn a simple, honourable grief to something shameful and humiliating. But it'll do

[151]

worse than that. Walter's a man who lives on his temper. He can't find his way in action unless he lets himself go. When something happens he's quite incapable of thinking it out quietly. He has to swear and storm and stamp about, and at the end of all the fuss some definite plan has crystallised in his mind, and he can get on with it. Madge doesn't care when he snaps at her, she knows perfectly well that at the bottom of his heart he hasn't a thought except for her and the children. But if you pretend to him that what he did in temper was of deadly importance, then you break his main-spring. He'll go about cowed and broken, he won't be able to stand up to life. That's the worst of you, Alice. You find out what people live by and you kill it.'

Alice said gravely, 'Jimmy, I don't understand this. Are you telling me that Madge and Walter have been talking against me? I've sometimes thought Madge wasn't quite loyal.'

'Oh, stop talking nonsense.'

'But you're being rude!'

'No loyalty can live near you. You are disloyalty itself. Of course we talk against you behind your back. We have to protect ourselves. You're out to kill your nearest and dearest. No, sit still. I've got a whole lot more to tell you. Do you want to know the real reason why you aren't welcome in Leo's house? You think it's because Evie's jealous of you. That is the most utter rubbish. The trouble about Evie, if there is any trouble about Evie, is that she's over-trained. She's had every instinctive naughtiness like jealousy educated out of her. If she thought your brother was fonder of you than of her she'd set her teeth and invite you to lunch, tea and dinner, at her house for every day of the week. But she knows that Leo can't bear you. Oh, he loves you, as we all do, because we know that apart from this devilish cruelty you're an angel, and because you've got this queer power of seeming a pitiful child that one can't help loving. But you frighten Leo. You see, he came back from the war after he'd been gassed, and forgot it. He felt splendid, and he married Evie, and they had four children. Then he had to remember he'd been gassed. He had that attack of pneumonia, and that slow recovery. And every day when he was getting better you went and saw him, and you sat and looked at him with those round eyes and asked, with an air of prudence and helpfulness that meant damn-all, "But what are you going to do, Leo, if you have a breakdown and have to give up your practice?"'

'Well,' said Alice, 'if a sister can't express her concern when her only brother's ill, I really don't know what we're coming to.'

From 'The Salt of the Earth' by Rebecca West, 1935

When Tess confessed to her husband Angel Clare that she had been seduced and had lived with her seducer, he sent her away. Now they have come together again.

She was so pale, so breathless, so quivering in every muscle, that he did not ask her a single question, but seizing her hand, and pulling it within his arm, he led her along. To avoid meeting any possible wayfarers he left the high road, and took a footpath under some fir-trees. When they were deep among the moaning boughs he stopped and looked at her enquiringly.

'Angel,' she said, as if waiting for this, 'do you know what I have been running after you for? To tell you that I have killed him!' A pitiful white smile lit her face as she spoke.

'What!' said he, thinking from the strangeness of her manner that she was in some delirium.

'I have done it—I don't know how,' she continued. 'Still, I owed it to you, and to myself, Angel. I feared long ago, when I struck him on the mouth with my glove, that I might do it some day for the trap he set for me in my simple youth, and his wrong to you through me. He has come between us and ruined us, and now he can never do it any more. I never loved him at all, Angel, as I loved you. You know it, don't you? You believe it? You didn't come back to me, and I was obliged to go back to him. Why did you go away—why did you— when I loved you so? I can't think why you did it. But I don't blame you; only, Angel, will you forgive me my sin against you, now I have killed him? I thought as I ran along that you would be sure to forgive me now I have done that. It came to me as a shining light that I should get you back that way. I could not bear the loss of you any longer—you don't know how entirely I was unable to bear your not loving me! Say you do now, dear, dear husband; say you do, now I have killed him!'

'I do love you, Tess—O, I do—it is all come back!' he said, tightening his arms round her with fervid pressure. 'But how do you mean —you have killed him?'

'I mean that I have,' she murmured in a reverie.

'What, bodily? Is he dead?'

'Yes. He heard me crying about you, and he bitterly taunted me; and called you by a foul name; and then I did it. My heart could not bear it. He had nagged me about you before. And then I dressed myself and came away to find you.'

From *Tess of the D'Urbervilles* by Thomas Hardy, 1891

She Asked Me To

I did not say anything, listening to the ocean sloshing against the pilings, feeling the pier rise and fall, and thinking that she was right about everything she had said.

Gloria was fumbling in her purse. When her hand came out it was holding a small pistol. I had never seen the pistol before, but I was not surprised. I was not in the least surprised.

'Here—' she said, offering it to me.

'I don't want it. Put it away,' I said. 'Come on, let's go back inside. I'm cold—'

'Take it and pinch-hit for God,' she said, pressing it into my hand. 'Shoot me. It's the only way to get me out of my misery.'

She's right, I said to myself. 'It's the only way to get her out of her misery.' *When I was a little kid I used to spend the summers on my grandfather's farm in Arkansas. One day I was standing by the smoke-*

house watching my grandmother make lye soap in a big iron kettle when my grandfather came across the yard, very excited. 'Nellie broke her leg,' my grandfather said. My grandmother and I went over the stile into the garden where my grandfather had been plowing. Old Nellie was on the ground whimpering, still hitched to the plow. We stood there looking at her, just looking at her. My grandfather came back with the gun he had carried at Chickanauga Ridge. 'She stepped in a hole,' he said, patting Nellie's head. My grandmother turned me around, facing the other way. I started crying. I heard a shot. I still hear that shot. I ran over and fell down on the ground, hugging her neck. I loved that horse. I hated my grandfather. I got up and went to him, beating his legs with my fists . . . Later that day he explained that he loved Nellie too, but that he had to shoot her. 'It was the kindest thing to do,' he said. 'She was no more good. It was the only way to get her out of her misery . . .'

I had the pistol in my hand.

'All right,' I said to Gloria. 'Say when.'

'I'm ready.'

'Where?—'

'Right here. In the side of my head.'

The pier jumped as a big wave broke.

'Now?—'

'Now.'

I shot her.

The pier moved again, and the water made a sucking noise as it slipped back into the ocean.

I threw the pistol over the railing.

One policeman sat in the rear with me while the other one drove. We were traveling very fast and the siren was blowing. It was the same kind of a siren as they had used at the marathon dance when they wanted to wake us up.

'Why did you kill her?' the policeman in the rear seat asked.

'She asked me to,' I said.

'You hear that, Ben?'

'Ain't he an obliging bastard,' Ben said, over his shoulder.

'Is that the only reason you got?' the policeman in the rear seat asked.

'They shoot horses, don't they?' I said.

From *They Shoot Horses, Don't They?* by Horace McKoy, 1935

The Death of Marat

The deed done, Charlotte waited impassively for her own fate to unfold. Caught virtually in the act itself, she had no desire to evade its consequences, only to explain clearly and coolly her motives. She had her wish. To Guellard she calmly explained that 'having seen that civil war was on the point of exploding throughout France and persuaded that Marat was the principal author of this disaster, she had wished to sacrifice her life for her country.' A committee of six further officials, including Drouet, the postmaster who had recognised Louis XVI at Saint-Menehould, continued their examination in Marat's apartment while they sipped refreshments. To this group Charlotte Corday admitted having come to Paris from Caen with the premeditated design of killing Marat but insisted (to the obvious disappointment of the investigators) that the design was hers alone.

As news spread quickly through the faubourg Saint-Germain, enraged and anguished crowds gathered, wanting to tear the murderess to pieces. One woman even said she would like to dismember the monster and eat her filthy body, piece by piece. Drouet could only dissuade them by reminding the crowd that they would lose 'the links in the plot' if they killed the principal miscreant on the spot.

In the Abbaye prison—the site of the first of the September massacres—Charlotte was taken to a small cell that had previously housed both Brissot and Madame Roland. She sat on a straw mattress, stroked a black cat and wrote a letter to the Committee of General Security (the police committee of the Convention). As if she were anxious not to be robbed of sole responsibility, she protested against

the rumoured arrest of Claude Fauchet, the Girondin deputy and constitutional bishop of Caen, as an accomplice. Not only had they not
concerted the plan, she insisted, but she neither esteemed nor
respected the man, whom she had always thought a frivolous fanatic
with no 'firmness of character'. In contrast, at many points in her
investigation, Charlotte stressed her own resolve and believed that the
common delusion that women were incapable of such acts had played
to her advantage. It was evidently a point of honour with her—and in
deliberate repudiation of the revolutionary stereotypes of gender—to
affirm that her sex was both physically and morally more than strong
enough to commit acts of patriotic violence.

From *Citizens* by Simon Schama, 1994

*The 'pitiless chess player', with the law on his side, manipulates men,
setting one criminal to kill another.*

'. . . You'd been watching Schmied for weeks, observed every step he
took; you were jealous of his abilities, his success, his education, even
his girl. You knew that he was after Gastmann; you even knew when he
visited him, but you didn't know why. Then by chance the briefcase on
his desk containing the documents fell into your hands. You determined to take over the Gastmann case and to kill Schmied, so that for
once in your life you would have a success yourself. You were right in
believing it would be easy to pin a murder on Gastmann. When you
saw the blue Mercedes in Grindelwald you knew what to do. You
rented the car for Wednesday night. I went to Grindelwald to confirm
that fact. The rest is quite simple; you drove through Ligerz to Scher-
nelz and left the car in the wood by the Twann River; you took a short
cut through the wood by following the gorge, which brought you to the
Twann-Lamboing road. You waited by the cliffs for Schmied. He was
surprised to see you and stopped. He opened the door, and you killed
him. You told me that story yourself. And now you've got what you
wanted—his success, his job, his car, and his girl.'

Chance listened to this pitiless chess player who had him in check and who now finished his gruesome meal. The candles were burning less steadily; their light flickered over the faces of the two men, and the shadows darkened. A deadly silence reigned in this nocturnal hell; the serving woman had disappeared. The old man sat motionless, hardly seeming to breathe; the flickering light crossed his face in waves, a red fire that broke against the ice of his brow and his soul.

'You played a cat-and-mouse game with me,' said Chance slowly.

'I played a game with you,' returned Barlach with a chilling earnestness. 'There was nothing else I could do. You killed Schmied and I had to get you for it.'

'In order to kill Gastmann,' added Chance, suddenly realising the whole truth.

'You've got it. I've spent half my life trying to corner Gastmann, and Schmied was my last hope. I used every trick in the trade to catch him—a noble animal after a raging wild beast. But then you came, Chance, with your petty felonious ambition, and destroyed my only chance. So I took *you*—the murderer—and transformed you into my worst weapon. That part was easy, for you were driven on by the desperation of the criminal who has to throw his guilt on somebody else. I made my goal your goal.'

'I've been through hell,' said Chance.

'We've both been through hell,' the old man continued with a dreadful calmness. 'Von Schwendi's intervention provided the final straw and drove you to extremes—in some way you had to establish Gastmann's guilt. Any deviation from the trail that led towards Gastmann might lead back to you. Schmied's briefcase was the only thing that could help you. You knew it had been in my possession, but you did not know that Gastmann had taken it from me. That's why you attacked me here on Saturday night. The fact that I went to Grindelwald also alarmed you.'

'You knew it was I who attacked you?' asked Chance, his voice lacking all expression.

'I knew it right from the start. Every move I made was made with the intention of driving you to desperation. And when you couldn't bear it any longer you went to Lamboing to force a decision with Gastmann one way or another.'

'One of Gastmann's thugs was the first to shoot,' said Chance.

'I'd already told Gastmann that morning that I was sending someone to kill him.'

An icy shiver ran through Chance and he reeled in his chair. 'You set us on each other like dogs.'

'Beast against beast,' came the pitiless reply from the other chair.

'You appointed yourself the judge and me the executioner,' hissed Chance.

'Precisely.'

From *The Judge and His Hangman* by Friedrich Dürrenmatt, 1952,

translated from the German by Cyrus Brooks

Thomas a Becket and the Servants of the King

FIRST KNIGHT: We beg you to give us your attention for a few moments. We know that you may be disposed to judge unfavourably of our action. You are Englishmen, and therefore you believe in fair play: and when you see one man being set upon by four, then your sympathies are all with the under dog. I respect such feelings, I share them. Nevertheless, I appeal to your sense of honour. You are Englishmen, and therefore will not judge anybody without hearing both sides of the case. That is in accordance with our long-established principle of Trial by Jury. I am not myself qualified to put our case to you. I am a man of action and not of words. For that reason I shall do no more than introduce the other speakers, who, with their various abilities, and different points of view, will be able to lay before you the merits of this extremely complex problem. I shall call upon our eldest member to speak first, my neighbour in the country: Baron William de Traci.

THIRD KNIGHT: I am afraid I am not anything like such an experienced speaker as my old friend Reginald Fitz Urse would lead you to believe. But there is one thing I should like to say, and I might as well say it at once. It is this: in what we have done, and whatever you may think of it, we have been perfectly disinterested. (*The other* KNIGHTS: 'Hear! hear!') *We* are not getting anything out of this. We have much more to lose than to gain. We are four plain Englishmen who have put our country first. I dare say that we didn't make a very good impression when we came in just now. The fact is that we knew we had taken on a pretty stiff job; I'll only speak for myself, but I had drunk a good deal—I am not a drinking man ordinarily—to brace myself up for it. When you come to the point, it does go against the grain to kill an Archbishop, especially when you have been brought up in good Church traditions. So if we seemed a bit rowdy, you will understand why it was; and for my part I am awfully sorry about it. We realised this was our duty, but all the same we had to work ourselves up to it. And, as I said, *we* are not getting a penny out of this. We know perfectly well how things will turn out. King Henry—God bless him—will have to say, for reasons of state, that he never meant this to happen; and there is going to be an awful row; and at the best we shall have to spend the rest of our lives abroad. And even when reasonable people come to see that the Archbishop *had* to be put out of the way—and personally I had a tremendous admiration for him—you must have noted what a good show he put up at the end—they won't give *us* any glory. No, we have done for ourselves, there's no mistake about that. So, as I said at the beginning, please give us at least the credit for being completely disinterested in this business. I think that is about all I have to say.

FIRST KNIGHT: I think we will all agree that William de Traci has spoken well and has made a very important point. The gist of his argument is this: that we have been completely disinterested. But our act itself needs more justification than that; and you must hear our other speakers. I shall next call upon Hugh de

Morville, who has made a special study of statecraft and constitutional law. Sir Hugh de Morville.

SECOND KNIGHT: I should like first to recur to a point that was very well put by our leader, Reginald Fitz Urse: that you are Englishmen, and therefore your sympathies are always with the under dog. It is the English spirit of fair play. Now the worthy Archbishop, whose good qualities I very much admired, has throughout been presented as the under dog. But is this really the case? I am going to appeal not to your emotions but to your reason. You are hard-headed sensible people, as I can see, and not to be taken in by emotional clap-trap. I therefore ask you to consider soberly: what were the Archbishop's aims? and what are King Henry's aims? In the answer to these questions lies the key to the problem.

The King's aim has been perfectly consistent. During the reign of the late Queen Matilda and the irruption of the unhappy usurper Stephen, the kingdom was very much divided. Our King saw that the one thing needful was to restore order: to curb the excessive powers of local government, which were usually exercised for selfish and often for seditious ends, and to reform the legal system. He therefore intended that Becket, who had proved himself an extremely able administrator—no one denies that—should unite the offices of Chancellor and Archbishop. Had Becket concurred with the King's wishes, we should have had an almost ideal State: a union of spiritual and temporal administration, under the central government. I knew Becket well, in various official relations; and I may say that I have never known a man so well qualified for the highest rank of the Civil Service. And what happened? The moment that Becket, at the King's instance, had been made Archbishop, he resigned the office of Chancellor, he became more priestly than the priests, he ostentatiously and offensively adopted an ascetic manner of life, he affirmed immediately that there was a higher order than that which our King, and he as the King's servant, had for so many

[161]

years striven to establish; and that—God knows why—the two orders were incompatible.

You will agree with me that such interference by an Archbishop offends the instincts of a people like ours. So far, I know that I have your approval: I read it in your faces. It is only with the measures we have had to adopt, in order to set matters to rights, that you take issue. No one regrets the necessity for violence more than we do. Unhappily, there are times when violence is the only way in which social justice can be secured. At another time, you would condemn an Archbishop by vote of Parliament and execute him formally as a traitor, and no one would have to bear the burden of being called a murderer. And at a later time still, even such temperate measures as these would become unnecessary. But, if you have now arrived at a just subordination of the pretensions of the Church to the welfare of the State, remember that it is we who took the first step. We have been instrumental in bringing about the state of affairs that you approve. We have served your interests; we merit your applause; and if there is any guilt whatever in the matter, you must share it with us.

FIRST KNIGHT: Morville has given us a great deal to think about. It seems to me that he has said almost the last word, for those who have been able to follow his very subtle reasoning. We have, however, one more speaker, who has I think another point of view to express. If there are any who are still unconvinced, I think that Richard Brito, coming as he does of a family distinguished for its loyalty to the Church, will be able to convince them. Richard Brito.

FOURTH KNIGHT: The speakers who have preceded me, to say nothing of our leader, Reginald Fitz Urse, have all spoken very much to the point. I have nothing to add along their particular lines of argument. What I have to say may be put in the form of a question: *Who killed the Archbishop?* As you have been eye-witnesses of this lamentable scene, you may feel some surprise at my putting it in this way. But consider the course of events. I am obliged, very briefly, to go over the ground traversed by the last speaker. While the late Archbishop was Chancellor, no one, under the King, did more to weld the country together, to give it the unity, the stability, order, tranquility, and justice that it so badly needed. From the moment he became Archbishop, he completely reversed his policy; he showed himself to be utterly indifferent to the fate of the country, to be, in fact, a monster of egotism. This egotism grew upon him, until it became at last an undoubted mania. I have unimpeachable evidence to the effect that before he left France he clearly prophesied, in the presence of numerous witnesses, that he had not long to live, and that he would be killed in England. He used every means of provocation; from his conduct, step by step, there can be no inference except that he had determined upon a death by martyrdom. Even at the last, he could have given us reason: you have seen how he evaded our questions. And when he had deliberately exasperated us beyond human endurance, he could still have easily escaped; he could have kept himself from us long enough to allow our righteous anger to cool. That was just what he did not wish to happen; he insisted, while we were still inflamed with wrath, that the doors should be opened. Need I say more? I think, with these facts before you, you will unhesitatingly render a verdict of Suicide while of Unsound Mind. It is the only charitable verdict you can give, upon one who was, after all, a great man.

From *Murder in the Cathedral* by T. S. Eliot, 1935

A soldier recalls what killing a man in war meant to him.

I have killed my brother in the jungle;
Under the green liana's clammy tangle
I hid, and pressed my trigger, and he died.

Smooth as the spotted panther crept my brother,
Never a creak of his equipment's leather,
Never a leaf dislodged nor bird offended.

With his palaeozoic prototype
My mother shared her own ungainly shape
In caverns on some slow Silurian stream;

And with the cublings played my father's sons,
Shoulder to shoulder chipped their flints and bones
Or scraped a greasy ichthyosaurus hide.

And, when the floods of purple slime receded,
My brother's hutments by the apes were raided,
I lay beneath my brother's legs and cried.

Yet I have fought my brother for the planets;
I have never stopped to hear the linnets,
Or watched the cocos grow against the moon.

I have only slain him in the shadows,
I have made his slant-eyed women widows
And inherited his empty meadows.

Denys L. Jones

Duty to a Totalitarian Ethic

Among his most outstanding characteristics were strict attention to duty, unselfishness, love of nature, sentimentality, even a certain helpfulness and kindliness, simplicity, and finally a marked hankering after morality, an abnormal tendency to submit himself to strict imperatives and to feel authority over him. The dilemma which confronted him, along with a large number of his generation, was that this tendency remained largely unsatisfied in a society confused about its values and inclined to deny them or admit them only shamefacedly. The military world alone seemed still to offer that firm and immovable world of concepts and values for which he yearned: comradeship, loyalty, honour, courage held good there in an absolutely direct and literal sense, unvitiated by differentiating glosses, which the simple, uncritical mind immediately felt to be 'subversive'.

It was this moral longing, as powerful as it was undirected, that made Rudolf Höss suitable material for the demands of the totalitarian ethic, because it contained everything he was seeking: simple formulas, an uncomplicated schema of good and evil, a hierarchy of normal standards orientated according to military categories, and a utopia. For him, unlike the majority of his fellow SS leaders, the demands with which he found himself confronted lay on a different plane from his personal impulses. Precisely because what he had to do seemed to him for a long time difficult, it gave him a feeling of particularly meritorious achievement. Again and again he emphasises in his life story how extremely difficult it had been for him, especially at the beginning, to be harsh, to watch executions, to see those who 'had run into the wire', to observe acts of brutality. He added that he was 'not suited to concentration camp service'.

In fact, however, this psychological feature was the very key to his suitability for his work, according to Himmler's principles of selection. Constant effort towards self-mastery continually stimulated his misguided idealism, so that in the 'cold, indeed stony' attitude which in his own words he demanded of himself, Höss could see the result of moral struggle. It was only through a continual process of hardening that he became the type of the passionless, fundamentally disinterested murderer to whom, beyond the given objective purposes, murder meant nothing. Hitler once stated that the expression 'crime' came from a world that had now been superseded, that there was now only positive and negative activity, and Höss was the product of this conception, standing outside all traditional moral categories, all personal contact with his acts. All consciousness of individual guilt had been eliminated and murder was simply an administrative procedure. In the type represented by Höss evil takes the shape of the uninvolved bookkeeper, pedantic, sober, accurate. Hate, he states, had always been alien to him, and in later sections of his autobiography when he repeatedly complains of his vain struggles with malicious, rough subordinates, there is no hint of retrospective self-justification. The man who attached so much importance to his bourgeois 'decency', who proclaimed his aversion from his comrades' alcoholic excesses, who stated that he never personally hated the Jews and had repudiated the anti-Semitic paper *Der Stürmer* because it was 'calculated to appeal to the basest instincts', precisely because of all this succeeded in becoming the 'ideal type' of Himmler's camp commandant, since any subjective impulse, from sadism to pity, would have disturbed the smooth functioning of the mechanism of extermination. 'As for me,' Höss told a comrade in 1944, 'I have long ceased to have any human feelings.'

From *The Face of the Third Reich* by Joachim C. Fest, 1963, translated from the German by Michael Bullock

For the Exaltation of Jerusalem

Then said Holofernes unto her, Drink now, and be merry with us.

So Judith said, I will drink now, my lord, because my life is magnified in me this day more than all the days since I was born.

Then she took and ate and drank before him what her maid had prepared.

And Holofernes took great delight in her, and drank much more wine than he had drunk in any one day since he was born.

Now when the evening was come, his servants made haste to depart, and Bagoas shut his tent without, and dismissed the waiters from the presence of his lord; and they went to their beds; for they were all weary, because the feast had been long.

And Judith was left alone in the tent, and Holofernes lying along upon his bed: for he was filled with wine.

Now Judith had commanded her maid to stand without her bedchamber, and to wait for her coming forth, as she did daily: for she said she would go forth to her prayers, and she spake to Bagoas according to the same purpose.

So all went forth, and none was left in the bedchamber, neither little nor great. Then Judith, standing by his bed, said in her heart, O Lord God of all power, look at this present upon the works of my hands for the exaltation of Jerusalem.

For now is the time to help thine inheritance, and to execute mine enterprises to the destruction of the enemies which are risen against us.

Then she came to the pillar of the bed, which was at Holofernes' head, and took down his fauchion from thence.

And approached to his bed, and took hold of the hair of his head, and said, Strengthen me, O Lord God of Israel, this day.

From *Judith* XXII

7

'A FIELD OF EVIL FORCES'

The Psychopath No One Understands

*W*oods had long suspected,' writes Norman Mailer in The Executioner's Song, 'the best-kept secret in psychiatric circles was
that nobody understood psychopaths, and few had any notion of psy-
chotics. "Look," he would sometimes be tempted to tell a colleague,
"the psychotic thinks he's in contact with spirits from other worlds.
He believes he is prey to the spirits of the dead. He's in terror. By his
understanding, he lives in a field of evil forces. The psychopath,"
Woods would tell them, "inhabits the same place. It is just that he
feels stronger. The psychopath sees himself as a potent force in that
field of forces. Sometimes he even believes he can go to war against
them, and win. If he really loses, he is close to collapse, and can be
as ghost ridden as a psychotic."'*

*Peter Sutcliffe, called The Yorkshire Ripper, believed the forces
which drove him on were divine.*

The doctors who had examined him, Sir Michael said, were all agreed
that Sutcliffe was suffering from the imbalance of the mind known as
paranoid schizophrenia. What Sutcliffe had told them, in effect, was
that he had had 'messages from God' to kill prostitutes and that what
he did was part of a 'divine mission', and the doctors believed him.

'But,' Sir Michael added, 'none of that detail was told to the police
at all.' Sutcliffe told the police he had had urges—hallucinations—but
of a different kind to the ones he described to the doctors and he did-
n't even tell the police that straight away. After his arrest, he had made
a statement to the police which it had taken the best part of two days
to write down. 'But that confession is curious, you may think. It is by
no means wholly frank. There were twenty murders and attempted

murders. He only spoke in his confession of fourteen.' Sutcliffe, when first arrested, did not in any sense say to the police: 'I have a divine right to do this. I am responding to God's orders.'

'What he did say, he told a whole series of lies as to how he had been caught and why he was in the car with a prostitute and why he had weapons in the car and why he had a rope in his pocket and gave a cock-and-bull story about how he came to be there.'

It may be, Sir Michael told the jury, that the discrepancies between what Sutcliffe told the psychiatrists and what he told the police were going to 'cause the greatest anxieties in this case and that they will be the most relevant facts to the issue of whether the medical evidence should be accepted by you or not.'

He emphasised that, while the Crown intended to demonstrate that Sutcliffe had 'duped' the doctors and was a 'sadistic killer', the burden of proving that he was suffering from diminished responsibility lay with the defence. Unless the defence could satisfy them that Sutcliffe genuinely believed that he had heard the voice of God while working at Bingley cemetery, they must find him guilty of murder on all thirteen counts.

The Attorney-General's opening speech continued late into the afternoon of the second day, when the first prosecution witness was called. Sutcliffe had told the doctors that in his late teens he had been involved in a motorcycle accident in which he had suffered a severe blow to the head, implying that this might in some way account for his later actions; and Donald Sumner confirmed that he had been riding pillion behind Sutcliffe on the night the accident happened. 'We had a puncture while we were going along and came off the bike. Peter went into a lamp-post and I went sliding down the road . . . Peter hit his head and was bleeding. There was damage to his crash helmet. He looked a right clown.' Sutcliffe had since claimed he was 'knocked unconscious for hours' and afterwards became prone to 'hallucinations and bouts of morbid depression—my mind was in a haze and I didn't know what was right or wrong. I didn't know whether I was acting rationally or not.' But, Sir Michael suggested to the jury, 'you may think he was embroidering this story.' (No member of his family has any recollection of the episode or can ever remember Peter injuring his head.)

From *Somebody's Husband, Somebody's Son* by Gordon Burn, 1985

A novelist imagines how a child without a moral sense might kill those who oppose or threaten her.

He threw back his head, and in triumph laughed his shrill foolish laugh, watching the child out of the corners of his eyes.

Rhoda got up thoughtfully and went to the lily pond, standing there with one foot on the rim of the basin; and then, convinced this time that Leroy told the truth, she said calmly, 'Give me those shoes back!'

'Oh, no! Not me, Miss Rhoda Penmark! I got them shoes hidden out where nobody but me can find them. I'm keeping them shoes to make you behave better from here on.'

He went into the courtyard. The situation had become too delightful for him to endure. He sat down on the back steps, rocking from side to side. The child followed him. She said patiently, 'You'd better give me those shoes. They're mine. Give them back to me.'

Leroy said, 'I'm not giving those shoes back to nobody, see?' He gasped with delight, holding his face in his hands. Then something in the child's fixed, cold stare caused his laughter to die away. He looked down uneasily at his own shoes and said, 'Now listen, Rhoda; I just been fooling around, and teasing you about them shoes. I got my work to do. Why don't you go about your business, and leave me alone?'

He walked faster, but she caught at his sleeve, pulling him up short. 'You'd better give me my shoes back,' she said.

He turned in exasperation and said, 'Quit talking loud. Everybody can hear what you're saying.'

The child said, 'Give me my shoes. You've got them hid, but you better find them, and give them back to me.'

'Listen, Rhoda! I haven't got nobody's shoes. I was just teasing you. Don't you know when anybody is teasing you?'

[173]

He went in the direction of the park again, but the child followed him insistently, saying softly, 'Give me my shoes. Give them back.' He picked up his broom where he'd left it leaning on the lily pond, and said plaintively, 'Why don't you leave me alone? What makes you keep bothering me?' But she would not leave him. She kept tugging at his sleeve and repeating her demand until Leroy said, 'I was just fooling at first about you killing that boy; but now I believe you did. I believe you really did kill him with your shoe.' He moved away once more, and once more she followed him; and then Leroy, as though he were about to stamp his foot in exasperation, said shrilly, 'Go inside and practise your piano lesson! I haven't got nobody's shoe, I keep telling you!'

He went to the front of the house, where he was sure she would not follow him. He stood under the camphor tree alone, saying to himself in amazement, 'I really believe she killed that little boy!' Then suddenly he said to himself, 'I don't want to have nothing more to do with her. If she speaks to me again, I'm not even going to answer back.'

He'd thought at first how interesting the story of the retrieved shoes would be for Thelma that night when he got home; but now he knew he'd never tell it to her or anyone else.

He was afraid of the child. He came to work next day determined to avoid her; to his relief, she did not come into the park that morning; but looking up from time to time, he saw her at her window. All that morning he was conscious that she followed his movements with her eyes, her head turning from side to side; and once, looking up quickly, their glances met. He turned uneasily away, aware of the unconcealed fury, the cold calculating anger in the little girl's face . . .

From *The Bad Seed* by William March, 1954

He had first intended not only to rob and kill Kinck but to assume his identity and to sail to the United States to begin life afresh there with money and a new name; but in the hurry, in the dark, he failed to bury his victims sufficiently deeply, and in pools shone their blood in the morning to lead the terrified peasants to the mass grave. Vanished with that discovery were all hopes of Troppmann's beginning a new life in the New World and quickly was he caught, his dogged ill-luck betraying him in the end. A policeman happened to glance towards him where he sat in a café in Le Havre, and such was Troppmann's agitation, the man suspected he had chanced on some petty crook and ordered him to come to the police station for questioning.

This last snapping of his hitherto iron will comes as a surprise. One had begun to feel that Troppmann, save for his own resentments and his gaudy dreams, was almost wholly inhuman; but at the last, after his Herculean labours, his courage suddenly went and he attempted to die, jumping into the sea. As the policeman led him from the café, he wrenched himself away and leapt into the dock; and only with difficulty was he rescued for the guillotine.

The abbé who attended him to the scaffold tells us that 'perpetually living in his imaginary world', Troppmann 'had lost all sense of right and wrong, and became filled with a burning desire to emulate those heroic criminals to rehabilitate their characters by giving the fruits of their crimes to the poor and suffering, and end their days by devoting to charitable objects an income that had been derived from the exercise of dagger and poison.'

From this dream of becoming a second, more benevolent Jean Valjean, murder was born. Thus does man sublimate into noble aspirations his passion for power, his revenge on society and his lust to kill, cherishing helpless animals because he wishes to feel himself the master of at least some living creature. Contrary to popular belief, criminals are commonly sentimental about animals, and Dickens remarks that he was surprised at the bad company birds keep. Troppmann's father was a dreamer, an artisan who, had he been given the opportunity, might well have become an excellent engineer. He did invent an improvement in spinning which was quite successful, but he was incapable of dealing with the world of affairs and he never did make the money a more practical workman would certainly have made with his abilities. The mother—and here we touch the nerve of young Troppmann's arrogance—adored little Jean-Baptiste, her youngest child, and drew him into her world of sorrows so that he grew up to share her feelings of having been cheated with a father, a husband who failed to become a millionaire, and would have become a millionaire but for the jealousies of a malevolent society, of that corrupt world under Louis Napoleon, in which financiers juggled, made and lost fortunes within a few days.

Rancorous, sullen, ambitious, violent despite his frail physique—which, in his determination to be stronger than others, he developed by exercising—Troppmann grew to manhood, concocting poisons in his home-made laboratory that, holding these deadly potions in his hand, he could feel himself rise above the inferior world, a dark angel of death who could slay with a few drops of his own brewing, like that angel in Revelation who poured out his vial, so that all on earth became blood. Yet even he, this classic murderer, could not confess to his personal hates or satisfactions in murder: even to himself, he had to pretend that he slew for noble purposes.

From *The Mainspring of Murder* by Philip Lindsay, 1958

A great psychoanalyst held a theory of an infant's 'phase of sadism'.

My earlier writings contain the account of a phase of sadism at its height, through which children pass during the first year of life. In the very first months of the baby's existence it has sadistic impulses directed, not only against its mother's breast, but also against the inside of her body: scooping it out, devouring the contents, destroying it by every means which sadism can suggest. The development of the infant is governed by the mechanisms of introjection and projection. From the beginning the ego introjects objects 'good' and 'bad', for both of which the mother's breast is the prototype—for good objects when the child obtains it, for bad ones when it fails him. But it is because the baby projects its own aggression on to these objects that it feels them to be 'bad' and not only that they frustrate its desires; the child conceives of them as actually dangerous—persecutors who it fears will devour it, scoop out the inside of its body, cut it to pieces, poison it—in short, compassing its destruction by all the means which sadism can devise. These images, which are a fantastically distorted picture of the real objects upon which they are based, become installed not only in the outside world but, by the process of incorporation, also within the ego. Hence, quite little children pass through anxiety situations (and react to them with defence mechanisms), the content of which is comparable to that of the psychoses of adults.

From *A Contribution to the Psychogenesis of Manic-Depressive States* by Melanie Klein, 1935

Porphyria's Lover

The rain set early in tonight,
　　The sullen wind was soon awake,
It tore the elm-tops down for spite,
　　And did its worst to vex the lake,
I listened with heart fit to break.
When glided in Porphyria; straight
　　She shut the cold out and the storm,
And kneeled and made the cheerless grate
　　Blaze up, and all the cottage warm;
Which done, she rose, and from her form
Withdrew the dripping cloak and shawl,
　　And laid her soiled gloves by, untied
Her hat and let the damp hair fall,
　　And, last, she sat down by my side
And called me. When no voice replied,
She put my arm about her waist,
　　And made her smooth white shoulder bare,
And all her yellow hair displaced,
　　And, stooping, made my cheek lie there,
And spread o'er all her yellow hair,
Murmuring how she loved me—she
　　Too weak, for all her heart's endeavour,
To set its struggling passion free
　　From pride, and vainer ties dissever,
And give herself to me for ever.
But passion sometimes would prevail,
　　Nor could tonight's gay feast restrain
A sudden thought of one so pale
　　For love of her, and all in vain;
So, she was come through wind and rain.
Be sure I looked up at her eyes
　　Happy and proud; at last I knew
Porphyria worshipped me; surprise

Made my heart swell, and still it grew
While I debated what to do.
That moment she was mine, mine, fair,
   Perfectly pure and good: I found
A thing to do, and all her hair
   In one long yellow string I wound
Three times her little throat around,
And strangled her. No pain felt she;
   I am quite sure she felt no pain.
As a shut bud that holds a bee
   I warily opened her lids; again
Laughed the blue eyes without a stain.
And I untightened next the tress
   About her neck; her cheek once more
Blushed bright beneath my burning kiss:
   I propped her head up as before,
Only, this time *my* shoulder bore
Her head, which droops upon it still:
   The smiling rosy little head,
So glad it has its utmost will,
   That all it scorned at once is fled,
And I, its love, am gained instead!
Porphyria's love: she guessed not how
   Her darling one wish would be heard.
And thus we sit together now.
   And all night long we have not stirred,
And yet God has not said a word!

Robert Browning, 1842

His illusory companion commands and instructs 'the highly favoured', inciting him to murder.

And then Gil-Martin (as this great sovereign was pleased to have himself called) frowned, and asked me what I was grasping at. I knew not what to say, but answered, with fear and shame, 'I have no weapons, not one; nor know I where any are to be found.'

'The God whom thou servest will provide these,' said he, 'if thou provest worthy of the trust committed to thee.'

I looked again up into the cloudy veil that covered us, and thought I beheld golden weapons of every description let down in it, but with all their points towards me. I kneeled, and was going to stretch out my hand to take one, when my patron seized me, as I thought, by the clothes, and dragged me away with as much ease as I had been a lamb, saying, with a joyful and elevated voice: 'Come, my friend, let us depart: thou art dreaming—thou art dreaming. Rouse up all the energies of thy exalted mind, for thou art an highly favoured one; and doubt thou not, that He whom *thou* servest, will be ever at thy right and left hand, to direct and assist thee.'

These words, but particularly the vision I had seen, of the golden weapons descending out of Heaven, inflamed my zeal to that height that I was as one beside himself; which my parents perceived that night, and made some motions towards confining me to my room. I joined in the family prayers, and then I afterwards sung a psalm and prayed by myself; and I had good reasons for believing that that small oblation of praise and prayer was not turned to sin. But there are strange things, and unaccountable agencies in nature: He only who dwells between the Cherubim can unriddle them, and to Him the honour must redound for ever. *Amen.*

I felt greatly strengthened and encouraged that night, and the next morning I ran to meet my companion, out of whose eye I now had no life. He rejoiced to see me so forward in the great work of reformation by blood, and said many things to raise my hopes of future fame and glory; and then, producing two pistols of pure beaten gold, he held them out and proffered me the choice of one, saying: 'See what thy master hath provided thee!' I took one of them very eagerly, for I perceived at once that they were two of the very weapons that were let down from Heaven in the cloudy veil, the dim tapestry of a firmament; and I said to myself: 'Surely this is the will of the Lord.'

The little splendid and enchanting piece was so perfect, so complete, and so ready for executing the will of the donor, that I now longed to use it in his service. I loaded it with my own hand, as Gil-Martin did the other, and we took our stations behind a bush of hawthorn and bramble on the verge of the wood, and almost close to the walk. My patron was so acute in all his calculations that he never mistook an event. We had not taken our stand above a minute and a half, till old Mr Blanchard appeared, coming slowly on the path. When we saw this, we cowered down, and leaned each of us a knee upon the ground, pointing the pistols through the bush, with an aim so steady that it was impossible to miss our victim.

From *The Private Memoirs and Confessions of a Justified Sinner* by
James Hogg, 1824

Small failings in the victim can be justification for killing, according to the murderous mind.

Dickie said absolutely nothing on the train. Under a pretence of being sleepy, he folded his arms and closed his eyes. Tom sat opposite him, staring at his bony, arrogant, handsome face, at his hands with the green ring and the gold signet ring. It crossed Tom's mind to steal the green ring when he left. It would be easy: Dickie took it off when he swam. Sometimes he took it off even when he showered at the house. He would do it the very last day, Tom thought. Tom stared at Dickie's closed eyelids. A crazy emotion of hate, of affection, of impatience and frustration was swelling in him, hampering his breathing. He wanted to kill Dickie. It was not the first time he had thought of it.

Before, once or twice or three times, it had been an impulse caused by anger or disappointment, an impulse that vanished immediately and left him with a feeling of shame. Now he thought about it for an entire minute, two minutes, because he was leaving Dickie, and what was there to be ashamed of any more? He had failed with Dickie, in every way. He hated Dickie, because, however he looked at what had happened, his failing had not been his own fault, not due to anything he had done, but due to Dickie's inhuman stubbornness. And his blatant rudeness! He had offered Dickie friendship, companionship, and respect, everything he had to offer, and Dickie had replied with ingratitude and now hostility. Dickie was just shoving him out in the cold. If he killed him on this trip, Tom thought, he could simply say that some accident had happened. He could—He had just thought of something brilliant: he could become Dickie Greenleaf himself. He could do everything that Dickie did. He could go back to Mongibello first and collect Dickie's things, tell Marge any damned story, set up an apartment in Rome or Paris, receive Dickie's cheque every month and forge Dickie's signature on it. He could step right into Dickie's shoes. He could have Mr Greenleaf, Sr, eating out of his hand. The danger of it, even the inevitable temporariness of it which he vaguely realised, only made him more enthusiastic. He began to think of *how*.

From *The Talented Mr Ripley* by Patricia Highsmith, 1956

That morning Mrs Campion had phoned Benfield. It was most important to prove that the photo of Myra on the Kilbride grave had been
taken after the boy's disappearance and not before, by establishing
that Puppet had been born round about that date, or after. Myra, suddenly vague about her darling, was inclined to think it had been well
before, and Mrs Campion had arranged for the dog (photographed
first, Leighton again) to be taken to Gorsey Lane Kennels to have its
age ascertained by means of a dental X-ray examination by an Edinburgh surgeon.

When Mrs Campion phoned, Talbot was with Benfield and could
just distinguish her voice, 'Oh, Mr Benfield, I don't know how to tell
you . . .' Benfield sat up, 'Yes, what is it?' Talbot couldn't make out
her answer but saw Benfield's face fall. 'Good God . . .' Talbot
thought, her husband, accident, hospital . . . Benfield turned to him,
'Puppet's passed away. Under the anaesthetic, now we *are* in trouble.'

And now, in Risley, two police officers faced the dog's mistress,
like shamefaced schoolboys, and blurted out the news. She stared at
them, incredulous and white with rage, then spoke a phrase which is,
deservedly, her last recorded saying in this book. 'You police are
nothing but murderers.' Her dog had died in Oldham Road, Ashton-
under-Lyne, three-quarters of a mile from John Kilbride's home.

When she has somewhat recovered and the normal careful interview
is under way, the two are behaving exactly as they will during those
seventy hours. Building up an image.

She looks straight at the solicitor, moodily; then, when he makes a
point, she takes her Biro and bends short-sightedly over her shorthand
pad, again as she did at Millwards and as she will in court. Where time
after time she will rise, lean over the dock wall and give an imperious
tap on the shoulder of one of the Defence lawyers; seven months ago,
if either one of the latter had paid an official visit to Millwards, she
would have been standing respectfully with the other girls. Having
made her note, she looks back at the solicitor, unblinking under level

brows. A faintly scornful stare which she has learnt from film posters and close-ups on television. An empty look. Imitation. Plastic Messalina. Talbot: 'Lookin' at her, you have to keep on thinkin', this is a girl who's lost her soul.'

Brady sits as he often sat in Number 16. And will sit, at the trial, when he will not be drawing rapidly on his pad—endless aboriginal profiles, villainous men with thick beards and brows in their eyes. One hand on the bony knee, the other holding the chin. A thoughtful intellectual onlooker who has lost interest. Born thirty years too late in the wrong country. Would have ended up at the top, Heil Brady.

She moody, he resigned. And in court the look will never change: continuously they will resemble a couple sitting in a register office who have come to be married, are being subjected to endless delay, cannot conceive what the red tape can be—all these folk natterin'— and are keeping their tempers with dignity.

To go further, they are carrying through to the end the fantasy of the Spy. For in their bearing, every detail is compatible with their being the Exiles who have Slaved for the Homeland, been betrayed by a Comrade, and are determined not to let down that Homeland with either doubt or fear. 'We report that in court today, our Hero and Heroine conducted themselves with exemplary dignity.' No medals though, the devil does not reward.

Only once will Hess let her Neddie down. One afternoon, descending to her cell after a day of horrors, she will glance up at a journalist looking at her over the partition, give him the stare, and then, for good measure, add the utmost vulgarity to the utmost injury. She will put her tongue out at him.

From *Beyond Belief* by Emlyn Williams, 1967

Whether or not 'psychopath' is a definition with any meaning, some have killed for no reason apparent to the ordinary man or woman. Wretchedly, they have often themselves not known why. Or they have dealt death for bizarre motives that seem beyond reason.

After counsel had made their closing speeches the judge began his summing-up, which . . . was detailed, painstaking and fair. But it was, as Dr Hobson says, 'stiflingly hot' in court and many people went to sleep, including Mr Curtis-Bennett who was heard snoring. At one moment when the judge was pointing at Christie and talking to the jury about 'doing justice' to him, Christie was observed scribbling a note to his solicitor. He passed this down and the solicitor read: 'I trust you did get a few cigs for me as I am absolutely out of stock. I feel OK.' Concluding his summing-up the judge said that 'putting it as shortly as I can' the issue before the jury was: 'Is it reasonably probable that when he killed his wife, Mrs Christie, he was suffering from disease of the mind producing a defect of reason, so that if he knew what he was doing, he did not know that it was wrong?' The jury retired at 4.05 pm on the fourth day of the trial and returned to court at 5.25. The verdict of guilty was hardly ever in doubt, though the time the jury had taken showed how carefully they had weighed up the medical arguments. Mr Justice Finnemore received the black cap, and in tears—for he could not help feeling pity that so dreadful a creature as Christie should exist, let alone have to die—pronounced sentence of death. Christie was taken down to the cells, the judge rose and left the court, the press hurried to the telephones, counsel gathered up their papers, and the great figures of law, literature and society went their different ways home. The most notorious murder trial in modern times had come to its end.

From *10 Rillington Place* by Ludovic Kennedy, 1971

The Russian psychopath, Chikatilo, holds the grim record of apparently committing more murders than any other known killer.

Once, during the years he was killing people, Chikatilo sought help. In the summer of 1984, when his compulsion to kill was so intense that he was murdering at the rate of about once every two weeks, he went to the clinic at Shakhty, where he lived. According to Dr Tkachenko, he wanted to consult a psychiatrist who worked there. But a *militsioner* happened to see him in the waiting room and recognised him.

'Why are you here?' the man asked. 'Alcohol?' It was the most common reason for a man of Chikatilo's age to go to the clinic.

The sight of a *militsioner* apparently unnerved Chikatilo. He left before ever speaking to the doctor.

His family life, meanwhile, was slowly deteriorating. In 1988, Pyotr Moryakov, his son-in-law, was hospitalised for a mental illness. Moryakov and Lyudmilla Chikatilo soon divorced. In 1985, Chikatilo's teenaged son Yuri developed a habit of taking the car jointly owned by his father and uncle without their permission. He drank, drove around, and had a couple of accidents. Chikatilo was forced to sell the car. Eventually, he began working on the strange little room in the middle of his apartment, the place where he would be able to retreat, undisturbed, with his fantasies.

Towards the end, he appeared to lose touch with reality. In 1989, Chikatilo began to be greatly agitated by the construction of the garage and the toilet in the courtyard by the apartment he was maintaining in Shakhty. It had been vacated by Lyudmilla when she remarried and moved to Kharkov, Ukraine. Feodosia wanted to keep it until Yuri got out of the army. Chikatilo wrote letters of protest to officials from Mikhail Gorbachev on down, complaining that the 'Assyrian Mafia' (some Georgians believe that they are descended from the biblical Assyrians) had bribed and corrupted the local government in an effort to despoil his living conditions. He travelled to Moscow and joined a protestors' encampment near Red Square. They were there to demand that the government do something to house Russian refugees from the growing ethnic conflicts in the Transcaucasus. That had nothing to do with Andrei Chikatilo's problems. Apparently, by that stage in his unfortunate life, he just wanted to cry out.

At home, he would later tell Dr Tkachenko, he read the newspaper accounts that began to appear about the *lesopolosa* killings. 'He was prepared for arrest for a long time,' Tkachenko said. 'He perfectly understood that sooner or later it would end.' Tkachenko had the impression that Chikatilo was anxious to unburden himself—that when the three *militsionery* finally surrounded him outside the children's café in Novocherkassk, Andrei Chikatilo felt something like relief.

From *Killer Department* by Robert Cullen, 1993

She asked for . . .

I run my metal comb through the D.A. and pose
my reflection between dummies in the window at Burton's.
Lamp light. Jimmy Dean. All over town, ducking and diving,
my shoes scud sparks against the night. She is in the canal.
Let me make myself crystal. With a good-looking girl crackling
in four petticoats, you feel like a king. She rode past me
on a wooden horse, laughing, and the air sang *Johnny,*
Remember Me. I turned the world faster, flash.

I don't talk much. I swing up beside them and do it
with my eyes. Brando. She was clean. I could smell her.
I thought, Here we go, old son. The fairground spun round us
and she blushed like candyfloss. You can woo them
with goldfish and coconuts, whispers in the Tunnel of Love.
When I zip up the leather, I'm in a new skin, I touch it
and love myself, sighing Some little lady's going to get lucky
tonight. My breath wipes me from the looking-glass.

[187]

We move from place to place. We leave on the last morning
with the scent of local girls on our fingers. They wear
our lovebites on their necks. I know what women want,
a handrail to Venus. She said *Please* and *Thank you*
to the toffee-apple, teddy-bear. I thought I was on, no error.
She squealed on the dodgems, clinging to my leather sleeve.
I took a swig of whisky from the flask and frenched it
down her throat. *No*, she said, *Don't*, like they always do.

Dirty Alice flicked my dick out when I was twelve.
She jeered. I nicked a quid and took her to the spinney.
I remember the wasps, the sun blazing as I pulled
her knickers down. I touched her and I went hard,
but she grabbed my hand and used that, moaning . . .
She told me her name on the towpath, holding the fish
in a small sack of water. We walked away from the lights.
She'd come too far with me now. She looked back, once.

A town like this would kill me. A gypsy read my palm.
She saw fame. I could be anything with my looks,
my luck, my brains. I bought a guitar and blew a smoke ring
at the moon. Elvis nothing. *I'm not that type*, she said.
Too late. I eased her down by the dull canal
and talked sexy. Useless. She stared at the goldfish, silent.
I grabbed the plastic bag. She cried as it gasped and wriggled
on the grass and here we are. A dog craps by a lamp-post.

Mama, straight up, I hope you rot in hell. The old man
sloped off, sharpish. I saw her through the kitchen window.
The sky slammed down on my school cap, chicken licken.
Lady, Sweetheart, Princess, I say now, but I never stay.
My sandwiches were near her thigh, then the Rent Man
lit her cigarette and I ran, ran . . . She is in the canal.
These streets are quiet, as if the town has held its breath
to watch the Wheel go round above the dreary homes.

No, don't. Imagine. One thump did it, then I was on her,
giving her everything I had. Jack the Lad, Ladies' Man.
Easier to say Yes. Easier to stay a child, wide-eyed
at the top of the helter-skelter. You get one chance in this life
and if you screw it you're done for, uncle, no mistake.
She lost a tooth. I picked her up, dead slim, and slid her in.
A girl like that should have a paid-up solitaire and high hopes,
but she asked for it. A right well-knackered outragement.

My reflection sucks a sour Woodbine and buys me a drink. Here's
looking at you. Deep down I'm talented. She found out. Don't mess
with me, angel, I'm no nutter. Over in the corner, a dead ringer
for Ruth Ellis smears a farewell kiss on the lip of a gin-and-lime.
The barman calls Time. Bang in the centre of my skull,
there's a strange coolness. I could almost fly. Tomorrow
will find me elsewhere, with a loss of memory. Drink up son,
the world's your fucking oyster. A wopbopaloobop alopbimbam.

'Psychopath' by Carol Ann Duffy, 1987

The Devil Came Up Out of the Ground

The man who murdered Katie Mason was a thirty-nine-year-old paranoid schizophrenic named Peter Carlquist. Two years earlier, he had been acquitted by reason of insanity in the attempted knife murder of his roommate, whom he accused of putting poison gas into their radiator. He had a long history of such attacks on people, including his sister and several high school classmates. As early as age six, he had told a psychiatrist that the devil had come up out of the ground and entered his body. Perhaps he was right.

Following the assault on his roommate, Carlquist had been institutionalized in a unit for the criminally insane on the sprawling grounds of the state mental hospital situated at the outskirts of the city visited by Katie Mason on that fateful July day. Only a short time before, an advisory board had judged him sufficiently recovered to be transferred to a unit housing an assortment of the mentally ill, where patients were permitted to sign themselves out for several hours at a time. On the morning of the assault, Carlquist strolled off the grounds, took a municipal bus into town, and walked into a local hardware store. After buying a hunting knife, he came upon the street fair. And there in the crowd outside Woolworth's he saw two pretty little girls wearing identical dresses. Somewhere in his deranged mind lies the secret of why he chose the dark-haired Katie to be his victim instead of blond Laura . . .

From *How We Die* by Sherwin B. Nuland, 1993

A gangster's anger and hatred will extend beyond the grave ...

For the second time he came up against her sudden irresponsible resentment. She was soft, she was dumb, she was sentimental—and then suddenly she was dangerous. About a hat, about a gramophone record. 'All right,' she said, 'go away. You've never given me a thing. Not even today you haven't. If you don't want me why don't you go away? Why don't you leave me alone?' People turned and looked at them—at his acid and angry face, at her hopeless resentment. 'What do you want me for?' she cried at him.

'For Christ's sake . . .' he said.

'I'd rather drown,' she began, but he interrupted her: 'You can have your record.' He smiled nervously. 'I just thought you were crazy,' he said. 'What do you want to hear me on a record for? Aren't you going to hear me every day?' He squeezed her arm. 'You're a good kid. I don't grudge you things. You can have anything you say.' He thought: She's got me where she wants . . . how long? 'You didn't mean those things now, did you?' he wheedled at her. His face crinkled in the effort of amiability like an old man's.

'Something came over me,' she said, avoiding his eyes with an expression he couldn't read, obscure and despairing.

He felt relieved—but reluctant. He didn't like the idea of putting anything on a record: it reminded him of fingerprints. 'Do you really,' he said, 'want me to get one of those things? We haven't got a gramophone anyway. You won't be able to hear it. What's the good?'

'I don't want a gramophone,' she said. 'I just want to have it there. Perhaps one day you might be away somewhere and I could borrow a gramophone. And you'd speak,' she said with a sudden intensity that scared him.

'What do you want me to say?'

'Just anything,' she said. 'Say something to me. Say Rose and—something.'

He went into the box and closed the door. There was a slot for his sixpence, a mouthpiece, an instruction: 'Speak clearly and close to the instrument.' The scientific paraphernalia made him nervous; he looked over his shoulder and there outside she was watching him—without a smile; he saw her as a stranger, a shabby child from Nelson Place, and he was shaken by an appalling resentment. He put in a six-pence and speaking in a low voice for fear it might carry beyond the box he gave his message up to be graven on vulcanite: 'God damn you, you little bitch, why can't you go back home for ever and leave me be?'; he heard the needle scratch and the record whir, then a click and silence.

From Brighton Rock by Graham Greene, 1938

Gary Gilmore was executed by firing squad in Utah in 1977. He had murdered two men after a quarrel with his girlfriend, Nicole Barrett. Laurence Schiller, who considered making a film based on Gilmore's life, put a series of questions to him.

WHY DID YOU KILL JENSEN AND BUSHNELL?
There is so much similarity between Jenkins [*sic*] and Bushnell: both mid 20s in age, both family men, both Mormon missionaries. Perhaps the murders of these men were meant to occur.

To answer your question:
I killed Jenkins and Bushnell because I did not want to kill Nicole.

WAS BUSHNELL A COWARD? WHAT DID HE SAY?
No, I wouldn't say Mr Bushnell was a coward. He did *not* seem a coward. I remember he was anxious to comply. But I don't remember anything he said except he asked me to be quiet and not alert his wife who was in the next room.

He was calm, even brave.

DO YOU WISH YOU HAD NOT KILLED BUSHNELL?
Yes.

I wish I hadn't killed Jenkins too.

DID JENSEN RESIST AND DID JENSEN SHOW FEAR?
Jenkins did not resist.

He did not show undue fear.

I was struck by his friendly, smiling, kind face.

DID JENSEN AND BUSHNELL DIE LIKE MEN? LIKE YOU WANT TO DO?
They showed no more fear than you'd expect from a man being robbed.

I'm almost certain they didn't know they were going to die until it was done.

DO YOU RECALL ANY FILMS OR NEWSREELS IN WHICH YOU'VE SEEN MEN DIE BEFORE A FIRING SQUAD?
Private Slovak—

Sure said a lot of Hail Marys, didn't he?

IF YOU HAD A CHOICE, WOULD YOUR EXECUTION BE ON TELEVISION?
No.

Too macabre.

WOULD YOU LIKE YOUR DEATH TELEVISED?
At the same time, I really don't give a shit.

WHAT DO YOU BELIEVE WILL HAPPEN TO YOU AFTER DEATH?
I could speculate, but I don't know—if the knowledge of death is within me, as I believe it is, I can't consciously bring it to the surface.

I just think it will be familiar . . . I must keep my mind singular and strong—In death you can choose in a way that you can't choose in life. The biggest mistake you could make when you die is to be afraid.

DO YOU FEAR WHAT A REINCARNATED BENNY BUSHNELL MAY DO TO YOU?
II have pondered that—But I don't fear it. Fuck fear. I may meet Bushnell—if I do, I will *never* avoid him. I recognize his rights.

WHY DID YOU KILL, AND COULD YOU HAVE STOPPED YOURSELF FROM KILLING IF YOU'D WANTED?

I never felt so terrible as I did that week before I was arrested. I had lost Nicole. It hurt so fucking bad that it was becoming physical—I mean I couldn't hardly walk. I couldn't sleep, I didn't hardly eat. I couldn't drown it. Booze didn't even dull it. A heavy hurt and loss. It got worse every day. I could feel it in my heart . . . I could feel the ache in my bones. I had to go on automatic to get thru [*sic*] the day.

> And it grew into a calm rage.
> And I opened the gate and let it out.
> But it wasn't enough.
> It would have gone on and on.
> More Jenkins, More Bushnells.
> Lord . . .
> It didn't make any sense—

From *The Executioner's Song* by Norman Mailer, 1979

The twenty-two years of his short life that Gary Gilmore spent in prison engendered in him a death wish that persisted until the end. His brother passionately wanted him to stay alive.

Imagine the impossible leaps and borders your heart must cross when you're arguing with a man about his own death. There was a logic, a congruity about Gary's choice, I had to admit, but none of that changed my desire for him to stay alive. But just as you try to convince the lover who no longer loves you to love you nonetheless—because you cannot imagine going on in your life, living it, without the presence or thing that you need and love most—in the same moment that you make your argument, and try to convince the person to stay and love you all over again, you also show that your argument is already lost, and along with it, a version of your future.

When you are arguing with somebody who is hell-bent on dying, you realize that if you lose the argument, there is no more chance for further argument, that you will have seen that person for the last time. I could not believe that I was in that place in my life, that I could possibly be caught up in such an argument. Death is one thing we almost never get to argue with. You can't argue with the disease that takes your loved one or yourself, or the car accident or the killer that snuffs out a life without warning. But a man who *wants* to die . . . When I argued with Gary, I was arguing with death itself—he was death, wanting itself as its only possible fulfillment—and I learned that you cannot win, that this thing which will ruin your heart the most cannot be resisted or stopped, that you will lose this person, and you will have to live with that loss forever.

From *Shot in the Heart* by Mikal Gilmore, 1994

Genene Jones's behaviour came in the categories of Munchausen's Syndrome and Munchausen by proxy, the former manifesting itself in her own imaginary illnesses, the latter in the sickness—and death— she arranged for the children in her care.

Like the women who harmed their own children, Genene appeared too devoted to her charges to harm them. When a baby died, her grief—the wailing, the singing, the cradling of the corpse—exceeded that of any mother. So devoted was Genene that she seemed to place herself above the parents. Of Chris Hogeda, Genene had said, 'He was *my* baby.' And she had condemned Petti McClellan's testimony as 'an insult to Chelsea's memory', as though Genene were better suited to judge.

Genene's personal medical history fit the Munchausen pattern as well: the repeated hospitalization and emergency room visits, the dramatic attacks of abdominal pain and breathing problems, the vague complaints of muscle weakness—'always acute and harrowing yet not entirely convincing'. Genene subjected herself to 'the more brutish hospital measures', but doctors usually could determine no cause of her problem. Several had labeled her a hysterical personality.

The quest for attention did not diminish after people began to wonder whether Genene was harming children. Instead of shrinking from suspicions—first at Medical Center Hospital, then in Kerrville, finally from criminal investigators and the press—Genene repeatedly tempted fate, daring her accusers to act, relishing the thrill of center stage. In the midst of the county hospital's internal inquiries, she approached doctors and asked, 'Do you think I'm killing babies?' At the meetings announcing the removal of the LVNs, she stood up and declared, 'It's me you're after.' In Kerrville, after Kathy Holland had confronted her with the bottle of succinylcholine, Genene orchestrated a dramatic suicide attempt, with a drug dose she knew would do no harm—if indeed she had swallowed any at all. There was the matter of her suicide note, with its suggestive reference to 'seven people, whose life I have altered'. After Holland dismissed the nurse, Genene's lawyer had advised her to leave the state; Genene instead relocated to San Angelo, just three hours away. And when made bond after her arrest, Genene moved *back* to Kerrville. Finally, there was her remark to Kathy Engelke, a stranger in the Bexar County Jail, who for some reason hadn't heard: 'I'm Genene Jones, the nurse that killed the babies.'

One child-abuse expert familiar with the case has likened Genene's behavior to that of a volunteer fireman who sets a blaze, then appears first on the scene in hope of becoming a hero by putting it out. In discussing the desire for a pediatric ICU at Sid Peterson Hospital, Ron Sutton suggested a motive that was but a manifestation of the syndrome. Still another theory is that Genene was playing, manipulating the health of children to satisfy a power complex, without intending to kill any of them.

In the case of this nurse who murdered babies, subtleties of motive are beside the point. Genene Jones's behavior defines her clearly as a psychopath. For her, the rules of society did not apply. For her, the lines between truth and fiction, good and evil, between right and wrong, did not matter.

From *The Death Shift* by Peter Elkind, 1983

Beverley Allitt committed similar crimes. While she was awaiting trial, her mind punished her body by devising new afflictions for it as she had devised afflictions for the children she killed.

It took a while for her to find herself behind bars. When she first arrived in the prison, she was quiet, overawed by her surroundings just like any other new inmate. They kept her in the hospital wing in case she tried to kill herself, saying it was a routine precaution which they took with anyone who faced such serious charges, although it was clear that they were concerned, too, that some of the other prisoners might convict her and punish her themselves. After a few weeks Bev began to find a role. She became louder, bossier, more bumptious. She found that most of the others on the hospital wing were weak, inadequate characters and soon she was the boss of the walk, referee of all disputes, keeper of the television controls, maker and breaker of friends, centre of attention. When her parents came to visit her at weekends, she was a jovial, back-slapping host, dispensing orders to the prison officers, calling up more cups of tea, lobbing jibes across the visitors' room at other inmates. She seemed impervious to her surroundings, quite undaunted by her fate. When she went to court for a remand hearing, she caught Judith Gibson's eye and flashed her a grin that made Judith churn with anger.

She wrote to Tracy asking her to visit, promising that she would swear in front of a priest that she had had nothing to do with attacking any of the children. When she received no reply she sent a prison probation officer as a messenger, but Tracy would not come. Bev heard that the police were planning to charge her with trying to murder Tracy's brother, but she still pleaded with her to visit and wrote sadly to another nurse to complain that Tracy had deserted her. 'So much for friends!' she said.

From time to time she went to the prison doctor: she had sprained her wrist, she had banged her arm, she had bruised her finger. Once or twice, she took too many sleeping pills. The hospital officers calmly absorbed her complaints and sent her back to the wing. Then, early in the new year, Bev seemed to grow bored with her bumptious, bossy role. Suddenly and decisively, she stopped eating. She said she could-n't swallow anything, she felt too ill, the thought of food just made her feel sick, she wondered if perhaps she had anorexia. The prison offi-cers in New Hall were not impressed. They'd seen it all before. They said she was just trying to con them. They said she was just looking for attention again—or, more likely, a transfer to hospital. And they were pretty sure she was sneaking Mars bars from other prisoners dur-ing association. They refused to play her game and simply continued to offer her food. Bev simply refused to eat it.

By June, Bev had lost four stone. She became so thin that the police were afraid she might be declared unfit to face trial, but a Home Office psychiatrist visited her and said she was healthy enough for the law's purposes. Then the game changed. Suddenly in late summer, Bev began to vomit, regularly and violently. The prison doctors could not understand it. If she was not eating, how could she have anything in her stomach to throw up? And what was making her vomit like this? They were sure she was not really ill but eventually, reluctantly, they gave in and transferred her to the local hospital, Pinderfields. They did so in a cloak of security—false name, false story, a guard outside her door—not so much to stop her escaping as to protect her in case someone found out who she was and tried to kill her. The doc-tors at Pinderfields watched her closely. The prison officers did, too. And after a few days they believed they had solved the mystery of her sudden vomiting, although the answer really only made the mystery deeper. They discovered that she was swallowing her own faeces. The discovery proved that the prison had been right all along—Bev was not really ill at all. But, in a sense, it proved the opposite—that she was suffering from some illness that was so profound that it beggared the imagination.

From *Murder on Ward Four* by Nick Davies, 1993

Dual Personality

I was stepping leisurely across the court after breakfast, drinking the chill of the air with pleasure, when I was seized again with those indescribable sensations that heralded the change; and I had but the time to gain the shelter of my cabinet, before I was once again raging and freezing with the passions of Hyde. It took on this occasion a double dose to recall me to myself; and, alas! six hours after, as I sat looking sadly in the fire, the pangs returned, and the drug had to be re-administered. In short, from that day forth it seemed only by a great effort as of gymnastics, and only under the immediate stimulation of the drug, that I was able to wear the countenance of Jekyll. At all hours of the day and night I would be taken with the premonitory shudder; above all, if I slept, or even dozed for a moment in my chair, it was always as Hyde that I awakened. Under the strain of this continually impending doom and by the sleeplessness to which I now condemned myself, ay, even beyond what I had thought possible to man, I became, in my own person, a creature eaten up and emptied by fever, languidly weak both in body and mind, and solely occupied by one thought: the horror of my other self. But when I slept, or when the virtue of the medicine wore off, I would leap almost without transition (for the pangs of transformation grew daily less marked) into the possession of a fancy brimming with images of terror, a soul boiling with causeless hatreds, and a body that seemed not strong enough to contain the raging energies of life. The powers of Hyde seemed to have grown with the sickliness of Jekyll. And certainly the hate that divided them was equal on each side. With Jekyll it was a thing of vital instinct. He had now seen the full deformity of that creature that shared with him some of the phenomena of consciousness, and was co-heir with him to death: and beyond these links of community, which in themselves made the most poignant part of his distress, he thought of Hyde, for all his energy of life, as of something not only hellish but inorganic. This was the shocking thing; that the slime of the pit seemed to utter cries and voices; that the amorphous dust gesticulated and sinned; that what was dead, and had no shape, should usurp the offices of life. And this again, that that insurgent horror was knit to him closer than a wife, closer than an eye; lay caged in his flesh, when he heard it mutter and felt it struggle to be born; and at every hour of weakness, and in the confidence of slumber, prevailed against him, and deposed him out of life. The hatred of Hyde for Jekyll was of a different order. His terror of the gallows drove him continually to commit temporary suicide, and return to his subordinate station of a part instead of a person; but he loathed the necessity, he loathed the despondency into which Jekyll was now fallen, and he resented the dislike with which he was himself regarded. Hence the ape-like tricks that he would play me, scrawling in my own hand blasphemies on the pages of my books, burning the letters and destroying the portrait of my father; and indeed, had it not been for his fear of death, he would long ago have ruined himself in order to involve me in the ruin. But his love of life is wonderful; I go further: I, who sicken and freeze at the mere thought of him, when I recall the abjection and passion of this attachment, and when I know how he fears my power to cut him off by suicide, I find it in my heart to pity him.

From *The Strange Case of Dr Jekyll and Mr Hyde* by
Robert Louis Stevenson, 1886

And Still He Wished for Company . . .

Another of the disquieting aspects of this case is the emergence of a motive which seems so bizarre, so incongruous, so unequal to the enormity of murder itself that it is almost insulting. We have already seen that Nilsen would often place a body on a chair in front of the television days after the death and then conduct a weirdly commonplace conversation with it, and also that he would carefully wash and dry the body to make it clean and comfortable. The stark, unpalatable fact is that Nilsen killed for company, to have someone to talk to, someone to care for. Nilsen's own explanation of his feelings runs as follows:

In none of these cases am I conscious of feeling any hate towards any of the victims . . . I remember going out to seek company and companionship, which perhaps would lead to a personal sexual and social relationship being established. On these excursions I cannot remember thinking about death, killing or past events. I was living for that moment only, and for the future. I would invite some people back with me, others would invite themselves. Sex was always a secondary consideration. I wanted a warm relationship and someone to talk to. Also I wanted to be a material provider and give hospitality. Because of the effects of drinking sex would (or would not) happen next morning. Through the night it is a nice relaxing feeling to have someone warm beside you in bed. I would never plan to kill anyone. In a sudden inexplicable act, I would be a bit dazed, shocked and shaking all over afterwards. I had a feeling of hopelessness, grief and a sense of emptiness, and even if I knew the body to be dead I felt that the personality was still within, aware and listening to me. I was the forlorn seeker after a relationship which was always beyond my reach. I felt somehow inadequate as a human being . . . Sex was not a factor of continuity with the victims (looking back and trying to work it out). The only similarity was a need not to be alone. It was to have someone to talk to and be with. They were not all homeless tramps, etc. Not all young homeless men who came to my flat were attacked or killed. Not all were even homosexual or bisexual. The reason that some were homosexual was mainly because they would come to the pubs which I frequented. I was approached marginally more times by those liaisons than I approached them . . . I sometimes imagine that I may have felt that I applied a relieving pressure on a life as a benevolent act, in that the subjects were ultimately freed from life's pain.

From *Killing for Company* by Brian Masters, 1985

The Boston Strangler

He seemed to regret especially the killings of the young women. About Sophie Clark, he said, 'There was no need for it to happen.' He denied suggestions that he had killed her to possess her. 'It wasn't the reason for having her. This is where the whole thing is messed up. There was no reason to be there, period. There was no reason for her to die. Nothing was taken away from her, no money, no nothing. How can I explain it to you? I'd sit there, looking to find something, looking through photographs like I was looking for someone.' About Patricia Bissette, he said, 'She talked to me like a man. I don't know why I did it. She did me no harm—and yet I did it. Do you follow me? Why did I do it to her? Why did I do it?' About the Joann Graff murder, during the traumatic days of the Kennedy assassination, he said: 'I cried ... when people started talking about how the President was shot—then, that he was dead. I just stood there and cried. Could the President be killed that day and I went out and still did something? Could I have shot out that way towards Lawrence that day, that afternoon? I heard someone say later it wasn't bad enough the President died but someone had to strangle somebody ... That Graff thing—it was senseless that it makes sense, you know? To me, it's unrealistic as to why these things occur.'

From *Hunting for Humans* by Elliot Leyton, 1986

When violence equals love in the disturbed mind ...

He thought of the chaotic scene at Bostwick Road—mother out at night, father married to his beer cases, shooting at trees and bailing out of moving cars. It must have been terrifying to a little girl. Had Virginia's instincts for survival led her to create a more satisfying internal world, albeit one that was purely artificial?

At the hands of her brother, father and school bus driver, she simultaneously must have begun to equate violent, foreign touching with love and attention. In her self-created reality, she converted these misdeeds into some misshapen form of love. And like most abused children, she probably began to believe that she deserved her mistreatment. Virginia began to hate herself.

Her continuous proximity to fires, shoplifting, and physical abuse also keyed in to a word Dr Tanay has used: *underaroused*. She needed the excitement of rule-breaking, Keeney suspected. The more brazen, the better the chance of getting caught, the more exciting. And she succeeded at her crimes, which led her to repeat them and take ever deeper risks.

By the time Virginia found Dick Coates, she had probably lost the capacity for healthy human contact. Coates was no more than a base for operations. From his home, she went out to sate her appetite for arousal: stealing food from Fran Newhart's store, clothes from town, and Mrs Pierson's silverware; carrying on illicit affairs. And she re-created the same unhappy, abusive life she had fled from at Bostwick Road.

Her precocious, trouble-making boys surely added a new set of strains. And so, over the years, her emotions receded further as she shored up the image of Virginia the Princess. At last, Dick Coates couldn't take it any longer.

Virginia fled to California. She might have made a break there with her ugly past. But suddenly she found herself knocked up with Cynthia Elaine. Bud Reardon came along and offered some respectability, but his sudden illness—just beginning at the time of Cynthia Elaine's death—and her two sons' burgeoning criminality led to a further retreat from reality. The moment marked the triggering point . . .

Had a little 'discipline' with Cynthia Elaine gotten out of hand? Or did Virginia vent her pent-up anger and self-loathing in one wild, uncontrolled burst? Or did she slip the child some of Bud's medicine?

However it happened, if she crossed that line and reduced Cynthia Elaine to an encumbrance to be disposed of, killing might have been one more way to find arousal.

From *Death Benefit* by David Heilbroner, 1993

8

'THE ONES WHO HAD TO PAY'

Murder for Murder's Sake

In life and in literature men and women have killed for the risk of it,
the challenge, or to see how they felt afterwards. Some seem to
have murdered for murder's sake, others because their victim
appeared at a crucial time and paid the price of an injury another had
committed. So it was in the case of 'Andy Reid'.

My biggest difficulty, it's living with myself, trying to come to terms
with myself, face what I've done. I took someone's life away;
because I didn't like the tone of his voice, no more reason than that.
Whatever he was, whoever he was, he hadn't gone out expecting to
get slaughtered for just saying something to someone as they walked
past him in the street. There's no way I can give him back his life or
make restitution. I used to think in prison because of that there was
no point in me being released. There was nothing I could do to give
maself back any worth. What I'd done was final, irrevocable, and it
wasn't done for any even faintly acceptable reason. Murder for gain,
people can understand that. Or murder in war, something deperson-
alised, they even invest that with a kind of heroism. You die for your
country, you kill for your country. That's very acceptable indeed, you
get medals for it and handclapping and cheers. You've killed people
for no reason other than you've been told to, your political leaders
tell you it's a good thing and want it done. Not what I did though, you
don't get medals or cheers for that. So where's the reality? I can't
connect it up. It makes no sense. I relive it time after time and it still
makes no sense. I don't make excuses for it, I wouldn't even think of
talking excuses; I never have. There's good murders and there's bad
murders, and this was one of the very worst.

It was late at night when I was walking along this street. I passed this man, I didn't know him, and just for a moment I couldn't believe what had happened. As I went past him he put his hand out and he patted me on the bum. And then he called after me, very softly, it was like invitingly, he called out, 'Oi, oi.' I can't stand things like that, I was wearing my knife and I turned round and stabbed him and went on stabbing him. I'm not saying I said it aloud, I don't remember that I did; but the phrase I was saying inside my head was, 'I'll kill you I will, I'll kill you.' People do say that. Out loud or inside their head. But not usually when they have a knife in their hand and are actually doing it.

I went back to where I was staying. I was staying with a relative or a friend. Actually she was both, she was the mother-in-law of one of my brothers. I'd been running, I was breathless, I was shocked. She asked me what had happened and I told her, and she asked me did I want her to send for the police. I said no I didn't, not yet, and she made me a cup of tea. Then I said I was ready: but she didn't need to send for them, I went to them myself.

. . . I'd gone round the night before to see them: my father'd been drinking as usual, and him and me we had a big row, he accused me of stealing money from him. I hadn't. I was angry with him, I went round to the house again the next night to have it out with him. It was late on, I'd had a few drinks maself in a pub before I went. When I got there he'd gone out, my mother said he'd be in some pub or other, it's be late when he got back so there was no point me stopping waiting for him. She knew there'd be another big quarrel between us if I was there waiting when he came back. She wanted me out of the house. She kept telling me not to stay but to go. In the end I said all right I would, and I went. I didn't tell her it was frustration, I was only going to go out and look for him, I knew the pubs he drank in, I knew I'd find him in one or other of them. I wanted to find him, I wanted to do him harm.

It was late at night and I was walking along this street. As I passed this guy he said, 'Oi, oi,' and touched me, and I turned round and stabbed him. I was looking for ma father really. It all keeps going round and round in ma head.

From *Life After Life* by Tony Parker, 1990

For a man who murdered a family, it was no more than 'picking off targets in a shooting gallery'. He was more concerned that his partner in the murders had run over the Clutters' dog.

Later, over cigarettes and coffee, Perry returned to the subject of thievery. 'My friend Willie-Jay used to talk about it. He used to say that all crimes were only "varieties of theft". Murder included. When you kill a man you steal his life. I guess that makes me a pretty big thief. See, Don—I did kill them. Down there in court, old Dewey made it sound like I was prevaricating—on account of Dick's mother. Well, I wasn't. Dick helped me, he held the flashlight and picked up the shells. And it was his idea, too. But Dick didn't shoot them, he never could've—though he's damn quick when it comes to running down an old dog. I wonder why I did it.' He scowled, as though the problem was new to him, a newly unearthed stone of surprising, unclassified color. 'I don't know why,' he said, as if holding it to the light, and angling it now here, now there. 'I was sore at Dick. The tough brass boy. But it wasn't Dick. Or the fear of being identified. I was willing to take that gamble. And it wasn't anything the Clutters did. They never hurt me. Like other people. Like people have all my life. Maybe it's just that the Clutters were the ones who had to pay for it.'

Cullivan probed, trying to gauge the depth of what he assumed would be Perry's contrition. Surely he must be experiencing a remorse sufficiently profound to summon a desire for God's mercy and forgiveness? Perry said, 'Am I sorry? If that's what you mean—I'm not. I don't feel anything about it. I wish I did. But nothing about it bothers me a bit. Half an hour after it happened, Dick was making jokes and I was laughing at them. Maybe we're not human. I'm human enough to feel sorry for myself. Sorry I can't walk out of here when you walk out. But that's all.' Cullivan could scarcely credit so detached an attitude; Perry was confused, mistaken, it was not possible for any man to be that devoid of conscience or compassion. Perry said, 'Why? Soldiers don't lose much sleep. They murder, and get medals for doing it. The good people of Kansas want to murder me— and some hangman will be glad to get the work. It's easy to kill—a lot easier than passing a bad cheque. Just remember: I only knew the Clutters maybe an hour. If I'd really known them, I guess I'd feel different. I don't think I could live with myself. But the way it was, it was like picking off targets in a shooting gallery.'

From *In Cold Blood* by Truman Capote, 1966

The two undergraduates in Patrick Hamilton's play have murdered a young man and later invited his father and aunt to dinner. The meal is served on top of a large trunk in which the body has been concealed. Finally, they confess what they have done to a friend and mentor.

BRANDON: . . . You are not a man of morals, are you?

RUPERT: No. I'm not.

BRANDON: And you do not rate life as a very precious thing, do you?

RUPERT: No.

BRANDON: Now listen, Rupert. Listen. I have done this thing, I and Granno. We have done it together. We have done it for—for adventure. For adventure and danger. For danger. You read Nietzsche, don't you, Rupert?

RUPERT: Yes.

BRANDON: And you know that he tells us to live dangerously.

RUPERT: Yes.

BRANDON: And you know that he's no more respect for individual life than you, and tells us—to—live dangerously. We thought we would do so—that's all. We have done so. We have only *done* the thing. Others have talked. We have done. Do you understand?

RUPERT: Go on.

BRANDON: Listen, Rupert, listen. You're understanding, I think. You're the one man to understand. Now apart from all this—quite apart —even if you can't see how we—look at it, you'll see that you can't give us up. Two lives can't recall one. It'd just be triple murder. You would never allow that. But apart from that too— our lives are in your hands. Your hands, man! I give them into your hands. You can't kill us. You can't kill. If you have us up now, it'd be killing us as much as if you were to run us through with that sword in your hand. You're not a murderer, Rupert.

RUPERT: What are you?

BRANDON: We aren't, we *aren't*, I tell you. Don't tell me you're a slave of your period. In the days of the Borgias you'd have thought nothing of this. For God's sake tell me you're an emancipated man. Rupert, you can't give us up. You know you can't. You can't. You can't! You can't . . . (*Long pause.*) Can you?

RUPERT: Yes, I know. There's every truth in what you've said. This is a very queer, dark and incomprehensible universe, and I under-stand it little. I myself have always tried to apply pure logic to it, and the application of logic can lead us into strange passes. It has done so in this case. You have brought up my own words in my face, and a man should stand by his own words. I shall never trust in logic again. You have said that I hold life cheap. You're right. I do. Your own included. (*Rises.*)

BRANDON: What do you mean?

RUPERT (*suddenly letting himself go—a thing he has not done all evening, and which he now does with tremendous force, and clear, angry articulation*): What do I mean? What do I mean? I mean that you have taken and killed—by strangulation—a very harmless and helpless fellow-creature of twenty years. I mean that in the chest there—now lie the staring and futile remains of something that four hours ago lived, and laughed, and ran, and found it good. Laughed as you could never laugh, and ran as you could never run. I mean that, for your cruel and scheming pleasure, you have committed a sin and a blasphemy against that very life which you now find yourselves so precious. And you have done more than this. You have not only killed him; you have rotted the lives of all those to whom he was most dear. And you have brought worse than death to his father—an equally harmless old man who has fought his way quietly through to a peaceful end, and to whom the whole Universe, after this, will now be blackened and distorted beyond the limits of thought. That is what you have done. And in dragging him round here tonight, you have played a lewd and infamous jest upon him—and a bad jest at that. And if you think, as your type of philosopher generally does, that life is nothing but a bad jest, then you will now have the pleasure of seeing it played upon yourselves.

From *Rope* by Patrick Hamilton, 1929

A stranger on a train was to be Lafcadio's victim, his death a matter of pure chance.

Lafcadio turned on the light. The train at that moment was running alongside a bank, which could be seen through the window, illuminated by the light cast upon it from one after another of the compartments of the train; a procession of brilliant squares was thus formed which danced along beside the railroad and suffered, each one in its turn, the same distortions, according to the irregularities of the ground. In the middle of one of these squares dances Fleurissoire's grotesque shadow; the others were empty.

Who would see? thought Lafcadio. There—just to my hand—under my hand, this double fastening, which I can easily undo; the door would suddenly give way and he would topple out; the slightest push would do it; he would fall into the darkness like a stone; one wouldn't even hear a scream . . . And off tomorrow to the East! . . . Who would know?

The tie—a little ready-made sailor knot—was put on by now and Fleurissoire had taken up one of the cuffs and was arranging it upon his right wrist, examining, as he did so, the photograph above his seat, which represented some palace by the sea, and was one of four that adorned the compartment.

A crime without a motive, went on Lafcadio, what a puzzle for the police! As to that, however, going along beside this blessed bank, anybody in the next compartment might notice the door open and the old blighter's shadow pitch out. The corridor curtains, at any rate, are drawn . . . It's not so much about events that I'm curious, as about myself. There's many a man thinks he's capable of anything, who draws back when it comes to the point . . . What a gulf between the imagination and the deed! . . . And no more right to take back one's move than at chess. Pooh! If one could foresee all the risks there'd be no interest in the game! . . . Between the imagination of a deed and . . . Hullo! the bank's come to an end. Here we are on a bridge, I think; a river . . .

The window-pane had now turned black and the reflections in it became more distinct. Fleurissoire leant forward to straighten his tie.

Here, just under my hand the double fastening—now that he's looking away and not paying attention—upon my soul, it's easier to undo than I thought. If I can count up to twelve, without hurrying, before I see a light in the countryside, the dromedary is saved. Here goes!

From *The Vatican Cellars* by André Gide, 1952, translated

from the French by D. Bussy

A Staffordshire Murderer

Every fear is a desire. Every desire is fear.
The cigarettes are burning under the trees
Where the Staffordshire murderers wait for their accomplices
And victims. Every victim is an accomplice.

It takes a lifetime to stroll to the carpark
Stopping at the footbridge for reassurance,
Looking down at the stream, observing
(With one eye) the mallard's diagonal progress backwards.

You could cut and run, now. It is not too late.
But your fear is like a long-case clock
In the last whirring second before the hour,
The hammer drawn back, the heart ready to chime.

Fear turns the ignition. The van is unlocked.
You may learn now what you ought to know:
That every journey begins with a death,
That the suicide travels alone, that the murderer needs company.

And the Staffordshire murderers, nervous though they are,
Are masters of the conciliatory smile.
A cigarette? A tablet in a tin?
Would you care for a boiled sweet from the famous poisoner

Of Rugeley? These are his own brand.
He has never had any complaints.
He speaks of his victims as a sexual braggart
With a tradesman's emphasis on the word 'satisfaction'.

You are flattered as never before. He appreciates
So much, the little things—your willingness for instance
To bequeath your body at once to his experiments.
He sees the point of you as no one else does.

Large parts of Staffordshire have been undermined.
The trees are in it up to their necks. Fish
Nest in their branches. In one of the Five Towns
An ornamental pond disappeared overnight

Dragging the ducks down with it, down to the old seams
With a sound as of a gigantic bath running out,
Which is in turn the sound of ducks in distress.
Thus History murders mallards, while we hear nothing

Or what we hear we do not understand.
It is heard as the tramp's rage in the crowded precinct:
'Woe to the bloody city of Lichfield.'
It is lost in the enthusiasm of the windows

From which we are offered on the easiest terms
Five times over in colour and once in monochrome
The first reprisals after the drill-sergeant's coup.
How speedily the murder detail makes its way

Along the green beach, past the pink breakers,
And binds the whole cabinet to the oil-drums,
Where death is a preoccupied tossing of the head,
Where no decorative cloud lingers at the gun's mouth.

At the Dame's School dust gathers on the highwayman,
On Sankey and Moody, Wesley and Fox,
On the snoring churchwarden, on Palmer the Poisoner
And Palmer's house and Stanfield Hall.

The brilliant moss has been chipped from the Red Barn.
They say that Cromwell played ping-pong with the cathedral.
We train roses over the arches. In the Minster Pool
Crayfish live under carved stones. Every spring

The rats pick off the young mallards and
The good weather brings out the murderers
By the Floral Clock, by the footbridge,
The pottery murderers in jackets of prussian blue.

'Alack, George, where are thy shoes?'
He lifted up his head and espied the three
Steeple-house spires, and they struck at his life.
And he went by his eye over hedge and ditch

And no one laid hands on him, and he went
Thus crying through the streets, where there seemed
To be a channel of blood running through the streets,
And the market-place appeared like a pool of blood.

For this field of corpses was Lichfield
Where a thousand Christian Britons fell
In Diocletian's day, and 'much could I write
Of the sense that I had of the blood—'

That winter Friday. Today it is hot.
The cowparsley is so high that the van cannot be seen
From the road. The bubbles rise in the warm canal.
Below the lock-gates you can hear mallards.

A coot hurries along the tow-path, like a Queen's Messenger.
On the heli-pad, an arrival in blue livery
Sends the water-boatmen off on urgent business.
News of a defeat. Keep calm. The cathedral chimes.

The house by the bridge is the house in your dream.
It stares through new frames, unwonted spectacles,
And the paint, you can tell, has been weeping.
In the yard, five striped oildrums. Flowers in a tyre.

This is where the murderer works. But it is Sunday.
Tomorrow's bank holiday will allow the bricks to set.
You see? he has thought of everything. He shows you
The snug little cavity he calls 'your future home'.

And 'Do you know,' he remarks, 'I have been counting my
    victims.
Nine hundred and ninety nine, the Number of the Beast!
That makes you . . .' But he sees he has overstepped the mark:
'I'm sorry, but you cannot seriously have thought you were the
    first?'

A thousand preachers, a thousand poisoners,
A thousand martyrs, a thousand murderers—
Surely these preachers are poisoners, these martyrs murderers?
Surely this is all a gigantic mistake?

But there has been no mistake. God and the weather are
    glorious.
You have come as an anchorite to kneel at your funeral.
Kneel then and pray. The blade flashes a smile.
This is your new life. This murder is yours.

James Fenton, 1982

A murderer who lives outside the accepted conventions of life talks to the examining magistrate.

Soon after that, I was taken to see the examining magistrate again. It was two o'clock in the afternoon and this time there was only a net curtain to soften the light which was flooding into his office. It was very hot. He made me sit down and very politely informed me that, 'due to unforeseen circumstances', my lawyer had been unable to come. But I was entitled not to answer his questions and wait until my lawyer could assist me. I said I could answer for myself. He pressed a button on the table. A young clerk came and sat down right behind me.

We both sat back in our chairs. The examination began. He told me first of all that people described me as being taciturn and withdrawn and he wanted to know what I thought of that. I answered, 'It's just that I never have much to say. So I keep quiet.' He smiled as before, remarked that that was the best reason and added, 'Anyway, it doesn't matter at all.' He stopped talking and looked at me, then sat up rather suddenly and said very quickly, 'What interests me is you.' I didn't understand what he meant by that and I didn't say anything. 'There are certain things,' he added, 'that puzzle me in what you did. I'm sure you'll help me to understand them.' I told him that it was all very simple. He urged me to go over the day again. I went over what I'd already told him about: Raymond, the beach, the swim, the fight, the beach again, the little spring, the sun and the five shots. After each sentence he'd say, 'Fine, fine.' When I came to the outstretched body, he nodded and said, 'Good.' But I was tired of repeating the same story over and over again and I felt as if I'd never talked so much in all my life.

After a short silence, he stood up and told me that he wanted to help me, that I interested him and that with God's help he would do something for me. But first, he wanted to ask me a few more questions. In the same breath, he asked me if I loved mother. I said, 'Yes, like everyone else,' and the clerk, who until now had been tapping away regularly at his typewriter, must have hit the wrong key, because he got into a muddle and had to go back. Still, without any apparent logic, the magistrate then asked me if I'd fired all five shots at once. I thought it over and specified that I'd only fired once to start with and then, a few seconds later, the other four shots. 'Why did you pause between the first and the second shot?' he said. Once again I saw the red beach in front of me and felt the burning sun on my forehead. But this time I didn't answer. Throughout the silence which followed, the magistrate looked flustered. He sat down, ran his fingers through his hair, put his elbows on the desk and leaned slightly towards me with a strange expression on his face. 'Why, why did you fire at a dead body?' Once again I didn't know what to answer. The magistrate wiped his hands across his forehead and repeated his question in a slightly broken voice. 'Why? You must tell me. Why?' I still didn't say anything.

Suddenly he stood up, strode over to a far corner of his office and opened a drawer in a filing cabinet. He took out a silver crucifix and came back towards me brandishing it. And in an altogether different, almost trembling voice, he exclaimed, 'Do you know who this is?' I said, 'Yes, naturally.' Then he spoke very quickly and passionately, telling me he believed in God, that he was convinced that no man was so guilty that God wouldn't pardon him, but that he must first repent and so become like a child whose soul is empty and ready to embrace everything. He was leaning right across the table, waving his crucifix almost directly over me. To tell the truth, I hadn't followed his argument at all well, firstly because I was hot and his office was full of huge flies which kept landing on my face, and also because he frightened me a bit. I realised at the same time that this was ridiculous because, after all, I was the criminal. But he carried on. I vaguely understood that as far as he was concerned there was only one part of my confession that didn't make sense, the fact that I'd paused before firing my second shot. The rest was all right, but this he just couldn't understand.

I was about to tell him that he was wrong to insist on this last point: it didn't really matter that much. But he interrupted me and pleaded with me one last time, drawing himself up to his full height and asking me if I believed in God. I said no. He sat down indignantly. He told me that it was impossible, that all men believed in God, even those who wouldn't face up to Him. That was his belief, and if he should ever doubt it, his life would become meaningless. 'Do you want my life to be meaningless?' he cried. As far as I was concerned, it had nothing to do with me and I told him so. But across the table, he was already thrusting the crucifix under my nose and exclaiming quite unreasonably, 'I am a Christian. I ask Him to forgive your sins. How can you not believe that He suffered for your sake?' I noticed that he was calling me by my first name, but I'd had enough. It was getting hotter and hotter. As I always do when I want to get rid of someone I'm not really listening to, I gave the impression that I was agreeing with him. To my surprise he was exultant. 'You see, you see,' he was saying, 'you do believe and you will put your trust in Him, won't you?' I obviously said no again. He sank back into his chair.

He looked very tired. For a moment he said nothing, while the typewriter, which had followed the entire conversation, caught up with the last few sentences. Then he looked at me intently and rather sadly. He murmured, 'I have never seen a soul as hardened as yours. The criminals who have come to me before have always wept at the sight of this symbol of suffering.' I was about to reply that this was precisely because they were criminals. But I realised that I was like them too. It was an idea I just couldn't get used to. Then the magistrate stood up, as if to indicate that the examination was over. Only he asked me in the same rather weary manner whether I regretted what I'd done. I thought it over and said that, rather than regret, I felt a kind of annoyance. I had the impression that he didn't understand me. But on that occasion that was as far as things went.

From *The Outsider* by Albert Camus, 1942, translated from the French by
Joseph Laredo

Gilles de Rais, Marshal of France, was tried for satanism, abduction
and child murder, and burnt at the stake. He is believed to have been
a model for Bluebeard. A poet conjured his dying words.

Marshal of France. The prancing horses
And banners licking the air. I tell you now,
Standing in pride who have no bright cuirass,
That was not half the glory, not a jot of it.
Now, velvet-draped like a coffin with nothing inside
But the echo of nails, remembering the hammer's
Talk in an empty vault, all I can do is tell you
God's mercy to me when I was alive.

I have seen angels marching—others also
Armed but all strong as morning, among the trumpets;
Though I am young, God's anger like a woman
Fought by my side three years, then was extinguished
In flame, the old sign, the old blazon shining.
It comes strange ways, the pure divine anger,
Piercing your safety like a lancet, or perhaps
A flat knife working for years behind the eyes,
Distorting vision. That is the worst of all.
Or a boy's voice flowering out of silence
Rising through choirs to the ear's whorled shrine
And living there, a light.

                    What if I sought that glory

When sign forgotten, fire had darkened my image
Of pure bright anger? What if indeed I danced
Another figure, seeking pain's intricate
Movements to weave that holy exultation?
Knife in the head before, now in the hand
Makes little difference. Pain is never personal;

[221]

As love or anger unconfined, it takes
Part in each moment and person, unconditioned
By time or identity, like an atmosphere.
There is no giving or receiving, only
Pain and creation coming out of pain.

Now I have made you angry; but think of this—
Which is the stronger, my pain or your love,
Old men like towers separate in the evening.

Six score in a year, I tell you. The high white bed,
Caesar's pleasures, and the dry well. See
How I believed in pain, how near I got
To living pain, regaining my lost image
Of hard perfection, sexless and immortal.
Nearer than you to living love, to knowing
The community of love without giving or taking
Or ceasing or the need of change. At least
I knew this in my commonwealth of pain.
You, knowing neither, burn me and fear my agony
And never learn any better kind of love.
Six score, then raising Lucifer by guile,
I sinned. It was unnecessary; so
It is for you to punish me. But remember
Never a man of you fought as I those years
Beside the incarnation of mortal pride,
The yearning of immortals for the flesh.
Nor will you ever feel God's finger
Probing your soul's anatomy, as I
Have been dissected these five years; for never
Since Christ has any man made pain so glorious
As I, nor dared to seek salvation

Through love with such long diligence as I through pain.

Have mercy, Lord, on misdirected worship.
On this soul dressed for death in hot black velvet.
Bishop of Nantes, cover the cross.

'Gilles de Rais' by Sidney Keyes, 1945

*And another who knew that man was a selfish, murderous brute, and
that the mind that 'is capable of reason also produces monsters'.*

It's true, no one has interfered with my freedom. My life has drained it
dry. A lot of fuss about nothing. This life had been given to me for
nothing. And yet I would not change. I am as I was made. But I can still
savour the failure of a life. After all, I have attained the age of reason.

But what kind of reason have I to assume that my gun will fire if
my finger pulls the trigger? What kind of reason to believe that if I
fired it at a brother's head it would blow his brains out? When I ask
this, a hundred reasons present themselves, each drowning the voice
of the others. 'But I have already done it myself innumerable times,
and as often heard of others doing the same. Why only the other day
there was an article in a magazine written by a former Mafia hitman
who used to shoot his victims in the head while they were eating
their soup.' (Well, at least I have the decency not to interfere with a
man's lunch.)

Reason is first in Nature, created that Man may investigate and
perceive and it is to be distinguished from Sensibility and Understanding. Of course it has a very natural tendency to overreach
itself, to overstep the limits of what may be experienced, and all
inferences which would carry us across the slippery ground are fal-
lacious and worthless.

And yet . . . the same mind that is capable of reason also produces
monsters.

There is an engraving by gorgeous Goya in which various creatures
of eternal night hover menacingly above the head of a sleeping man—

perhaps Goya himself: certainly there are few artists who can rival his monstrous imaginings. These monsters in the engraving are, of course, symbolic. The real monster, as Hobbes tells us (and, for that matter Freud), is Man himself—a savage, selfish, murderous brute. Society, says Hobbes, exists so that man may leave his brutish nature chained up at home, that he may aspire to something greater.

But if Man's original state is to be asocial and destructively rapacious then if he aspires to go beyond this state, does he grow nearer to God, or does he find himself growing further away?

For my own part I find the aspects of my character which are solitary, poor, nasty, brutish and short are far stronger than those civilising constraints which are imposed by society. I find that I understand, only too well, those who are at war against the world.

We all look to fathom the mind of a mass-murderer and to understand what makes him commit such heinous crimes.

Yet which of us can honestly say that in his Hobbesian heart of hearts, he does not already have the answer?

From *A Philosophical Investigation* by Philip Kerr, 1992

A Killer Like a Child

She was as silent as a stone woman.

'All right,' I went on heavily. 'Will you take her away? Somewhere far off from here where they can handle her type, where they will keep guns and knives and fancy drinks away from her? Hell, she might even get herself cured, you know. It's been done.'

She got up and walked slowly to the windows. The drapes lay in heavy ivory folds beside her feet. She stood among the folds and looked out, towards the quiet darkish foothills. Her hands hung loose at her sides. Utterly motionless hands. She turned and came back along the room and walked past me blindly. When she was behind me she caught her breath sharply and spoke.

'He's in the sump,' she said. 'A horrible decayed thing. I did it. I did just what you said. I went to Eddie Mars. She came home and told me about it, just like a child. She's not normal. I knew the police would get it all out of her. In a little while she would even brag about it. And if dad knew, he would call them instantly and tell them the whole story. And some time in that night he would die. It's not his dying—it's what he would be thinking just before he died. Rusty wasn't a bad fellow. I didn't love him. He was all right, I guess. He just didn't mean anything to me, one way or another, alive or dead, compared with keeping it from dad.'

'So you let her run around loose,' I said, 'getting into other jams.'

'I was playing for time. Just for time. I played the wrong way, of course. I thought she might even forget it herself. I've heard they do forget what happens in those fits. Maybe she has forgotten it. I knew Eddie Mars would bleed me white, but I didn't care. I had to have help and I could only get it from somebody like him . . . There have been times when I hardly believed it all myself. And other times when I had to get drunk quickly—whatever time of day it was. Awfully damn quickly.'

'You'll take her away,' I said. 'And do that awfully damn quickly.'

From *The Big Sleep* by Raymond Chandler, 1939

From New York hoodlum, Billy the Kid became the most feared man of the whole frontier, projecting the hatred he felt for one minority group on to another.

The boy of the sewer and the knock on the head rose to become a man of the frontier. He made a horseman of himself, learning to ride straight in the saddle—Wyoming- or Texas-style—and not with his body thrown back, the way they ride in Oregon and California. He never completely matched his legend, but he kept getting closer and closer to it. Something of the New York hoodlum lived on in the cowboy; he transferred to Mexicans the hatred that had previously been inspired in him by Negroes, but the last words he ever spoke were (swear) words in Spanish. He learned the art of the cowpuncher's maverick life. He learned another, more difficult art—how to lead men. Both helped to make him a good cattle rustler. From time to time, Old Mexico's guitars and whorehouses pulled on him.

With the haunting lucidity of insomnia, he organized populous orgies that often lasted four days and four nights. In the end, glutted, he settled accounts with bullets. While his trigger finger was unfailing, he was the most feared man (and perhaps the most anonymous and most lonely) of that whole frontier. Pat Garrett, his friend, the sheriff who later killed him, once told him, 'I've had a lot of practice with the rifle shooting buffalo.'

'I've had plenty with the six-shooter,' Billy replied modestly. 'Shooting tin cans and men.'

The details can never be recovered, but it is known that he was credited with up to twenty-one killings—'not counting Mexicans'. For seven desperate years, he practised the extravagance of utter recklessness.

The night of the twenty-fifth of July 1880, Billy the Kid came galloping on his piebald down the main, or only, street of Fort Sumner. The heat was oppressive and the lamps had not been lighted; Sheriff Garrett, seated on a porch in a rocking chair, drew his revolver and sent a bullet through the Kid's belly. The horse kept on; the rider tumbled into the dust of the road. Garrett got off a second shot. The townspeople (knowing the wounded man was Billy the Kid) locked their window shutters tight. The agony was long and blasphemous. In the morning, the sun by then high overhead, they began drawing near, and they disarmed him. The man was gone. They could see in his face that used-up look of the dead.

From *The Disinterested Killer Bill Harrigan* by Jorge Luis Borges, 1954, translated from the Spanish by Norman Thomas di Giovanni

Unreasoned murder may bring its own satisfaction . . .

He walked even closer, so that his shoulder touched Mike's arm. 'I never been to a lynching. How's it make you feel—afterwards?'

Mike shied away from the contact. 'It don't make you feel nothing.' He put down his head and increased his pace. The little bartender had nearly to trot to keep up. The street lights were fewer. It was darker and safer. Mike burst out, 'Makes you feel kind of cut off and tired, but kind of satisfied, too. Like you done a good job—but tired and kind of sleepy.' He slowed his steps. 'Look, there's a light in the kitchen. That's where I live. My old lady's waiting up for me.' He stopped in front of his little house.

Welch stood nervously beside him. 'Come into my place when you want a glass of beer—or a shot. Open 'til midnight. I treat my friends right.' He scampered away like an aged mouse.

Mike called, 'Good night.'

He walked round the side of his house and went in the back door. His thin petulant wife was sitting by the open gas stove warming herself. She turned complaining eyes on Mike where he stood in the door.

Then her eyes widened and hung on his face. 'You been with a woman,' she said hoarsely. 'What woman you been with?'

Mike laughed. 'You think you're pretty slick, don't you? You're a slick one, ain't you? What makes you think I been with a woman?'

She said fiercely, 'You think I can't tell by the look on your face that you been with a woman?'

'All right,' said Mike. 'If you're so slick and know-it-all, I won't tell you nothing. You can just wait for the morning paper.'

He saw doubt come into the dissatisfied eyes. 'Was it the nigger?' she asked. 'Did they get the nigger? Everybody said they was going to.'

'Find out for yourself if you're so slick. I ain't going to tell you nothing.'

He walked through the kitchen and went into the bathroom. A little mirror hung on the wall. Mike took off his cap and looked at his face. 'By God, she was right,' he thought. 'That's exactly how I do feel.'

From 'The Lonesome Vigilante' by John Steinbeck, 1940

Kafka only hints at the motive for Schmar's killing of Wese, while suggesting that it was primarily a murder for relief and release.

'Done,' said Schmar, and pitched the knife, now superfluous blood-stained ballast, against the nearest house front. 'The bliss of murder! The relief, the soaring ecstasy from the shedding of another's blood! Wese, old nightbird, friend, alehouse crony, you are oozing away into the dark earth below the street. Why aren't you simply a bladder of blood so that I could stamp on you and make you vanish into nothingness. Not all we want comes true, not all the dreams that blossomed have borne fruit, your solid remains lie here, already indifferent to every kick. What's the good of the dumb question you are asking?'

Pallas, choking on the poison in his body, stood at the double-leafed door of his house as it flew open. 'Schmar! Schmar! I saw it all, I missed nothing.' Pallas and Schmar scrutinised each other. The result of the scrutiny satisfied Pallas, Schmar came to no conclusion.

Mrs Wese, with a crowd of people on either side, came rushing up, her face grown quite old from the shock. Her fur coat swung open, she collapsed on top of Wese, the nightgowned body belonged to Wese, the fur coat spreading over the couple like the smooth turf of a grave

[228]

belonged to the crowd. Schmar, fighting with difficulty the last of his nausea, pressed his mouth against the shoulder of the policeman who, stepping lightly, led him away.

From 'A Fratricide' by Franz Kafka (1883–1924), translated from the German by
Willa and Edwin Muir

The final extract in this book is taken from Denis Nilsen's unpublished memoir, The Psychograph. *It was written in prison and has been cut but not otherwise edited or emended. A revelation of the psychological processes of someone who killed out of loneliness and despair, it shows how a man may react to panic and 'the long cold night'.*

He fought a grim realisation that a fantasy was not enough and that he needed the warmth of mutual viability. He wasn't getting any younger. One night he 'picked up' a rootless young man outside of a Gay Pub after closing time and took him home. The eighteen-year-old youth had no plans for the future other than where his next meal was coming from. He was easily persuaded to set up home with Sixten in a new flatlet. Sixten invested his meagre financial resources on a good hope for the future. After the initial 'honeymoon' period the youth lapsed back into his wandering ways and kept irregular hours with scant regard for all the domestic, as well as emotional responsibilities of a relationship. He would bring casual pick-ups back to the flat or spend days away with men who had picked him up in Central London. Sixten tolerated it for about eighteen months and had, himself, sought solace back inside the Gay Scene. Soon his partner found a rich 'sugardaddie' and left Sixten to be a live-in bumboy in the Mayfair area. It was a return to the field of domestic loneliness for Sixten.

In the next eighteen months he had other short term casual liaisons which left him nothing more substantial than mildly routine venereal disease. (With thefts of his money and property.) He was accumulating more problems as time drifted through the year until Christmas.

The problems by themselves in manageable proportions could be weathered within the ups and downs of life. However, Sixten's social and psychological landscape became dangerously barren with the long strain of a congruence of many problems in full concentrated force. It was 1978.

The manifold points of convergence encompassed all sectors of his life. His domestic security was under threat as the owners of the large house containing his flatlet had, ominously, expressed that, in order to sell the house, they wished to have vacant possession of it. (They made it clear that they wished that Sixten should move out. Two years later an intruder entered with a key and destroyed all of his possessions and electrical equipment.)

He was often robbed by some of his nocturnal 'pick-ups' and had his beloved sound movie camera and film projector stolen. On a couple of more public occasions he was 'Gay-bashed' and robbed. The house began to empty as outgoing tenants were not replaced according to the policy of the Landlord. High rents, prices (in a rapidly expanding inflation rate) and low clerical wages always left him short of money, a situation aggravated by his increasing reliance on strong drink. The whole house took on the appearance of a run down slum as the front windows were boarded up and no routine repairs had been done to the property for several years. His 'relationship' with his former colleagues in the local police had sunk to zero, with active hostility against him when it became widely known that he was 'Queer'. (He had already been arrested and abused at the local police station and falsely accused of sexually assaulting a seventeen-year-old youth a couple of years previously.)

His years of voluntary work as a trades union official were a thankless series of setbacks and defeats for a general membership who only cared for the immediate convenience of self-interest at the expense of any democratic principles. They wanted him to do 'the dirty work' of representation and 'take management stick', but offered him no real practical backing. Management regarded him as a thorn in their sides and repeatedly gave him promotionally bad adverse annual reports on the official grounds of his 'personality and attitude'. He was never recommended for promotion whilst other less skilled, pliant individuals with the 'right attitude' were frequently given executive grade over him. It was easy to interpret his 'bad personality' in terms of official homophobia. (Everybody knew he was Gay and he made no secret of it. He was never demonstrably florid in his sexual orientation and, in dress and manner, he appeared to be a conservative heterosexual; so much for appearances.) His bad 'attitude' as perceived by officials was clearly his scrupulous attention in serving his union duties which was not always sympathetic to official policies. (He was no 'Management Patsy' using the union to advance his own career, which was such a common feature of many civil servants.) Added to this was the Communist/Militant/Marxist/Trotskyite Union Tendancy which regarded him as a 'Fascist' and the Union Right Wing suspicion that he was a Communist. Tribalism demands that you must be in one camp or the other. He was nobody's man; not even his own. It was also a time of 'The winter of discontent' with failed Labour Government and TUC policies and the extremely dark spectre of 'Thatcherism' hanging over the horizon.

Inside the whole conundrum of despair was a trauma more significantly depressive than all the rest. Sixten had to kill his 'children'. His only remaining friend was his four-year-old sheepdog/terrier bitch, whose canine paramours still managed to climb the garden's seven-foot paling fence and make her pregnant. Initially, Sixten had found homes for the pups, especially through the local pet shop. Latterly there seemed to be a glut of unwanted puppies and, as they passed the seven-week-old mark when the bitch began to reject them, he was faced with an awesome decision. After much dilemmic delay he got himself very drunk, in order to remove inhibition, and drowned them all in his kitchen sink. He felt like a murderer and became fitfully depressed and tearful at acts which he regarded as the worst things he had ever done in his life. He never managed to shake off the guilt and memory of the scene and, to alleviate the unquenchable pain he turned more and more to the bottle. Yes, he had murdered his 'children' and the unthinkable situation seemed to climax into numbed nothingness.

The final and fatal images of what would be a ritualised tableau of smothering death crept closely on the heels of the dying year. Sixten spent Christmas alone, sitting inside the vacancy of his hopes, with the tinkling drowsy noise and colour of seasonal jingles on the large TV screen. In the daze cycled solitude he sat holding his dog as blank incomprehension unfolded deeper into the next glass of Bacardi and Coke. Like an addict he plugged into his stereo and released the grand flourish of the second half of Rachmaninov's Symphony No. 1. Inside the drunken grip of fantasy he drifted out to the local 'rough-house' public house and there, inside the land of false smiles, stood the boy of his dreams. It was a scene out of focus save for the clear image of the 'magic two'. There followed a blurred affinity of union. They lay naked and entwined inside the warm fur of secure thoughts, into the early hours of Hogmany. Sixten wanted it to go on into eternity. He was loved, warm and safe from the long cold night.

As threatening dawn approached he knew that this lovely, nameless figure beside him would leave as others had always left him. He was seized by a sudden panic and he was embraced by an irresistible frissive effort into ensuring that his dream-mate would stay with him forever. In the desperate heat of thirty years of stumbling frustration he stopped the youth awaking into a personality which would subvert his longings. By almost instinctive super-power energy he smothered the boy into permanent passivity. Sixten's maladjusted psychograph had rendered the man into a lifeless prop and himself into a killer of men.

From *The Psychograph* by Denis Nilsen

ACKNOWLEDGEMENTS

The editor and publishers gratefully acknowledge permission to reprint copyright materials as follows:

The extract from *The Book of Evidence*, copyright © 1989 by John Banville, reprinted by permission of Martin Secker & Warburg Ltd; the excerpt from 'The Disinterested Killer Bill Harrigan' from *A Universal History of Infamy* by Jorge Luis Borges, translated by Norman Thomas di Giovanni, translation copyright © 1970, 1971, 1972 by Emece Editores, S. A. and Norman Thomas di Giovanni, used by permission of Dutton Signet, a division of Penguin Books USA Inc. The excerpt from *Collected Stories* by Elizabeth Bowen, copyright © 1981 by Curtis Brown Ltd, Literary Executors of the Estate of Elizabeth Bowen, reprinted by permission of Alfred A. Knopf, Inc. and Random House UK Ltd; the excerpt from *Somebody's Husband, Somebody's Son* by Gordon Burn, reprinted by permission of the author and William Heinemann Ltd; the excerpt from *Double Indemnity* by James M. Cain copyright © 1943 by Alfred A. Knopf, Inc. and reprinted by permission of the publisher; the excerpt from *The Outsider* by Albert Camus, the translation copyright © 1982 by Joseph Laredo, reprinted by permission of Alfred A. Knopf, Inc. and Penguin Books Ltd; the excerpt from *In Cold Blood* copyright © 1966 by Truman Capote, reprinted by permission of Alfred A. Knopf, Inc.; 'All the Better to See You With', from *Belfast Confetti* by Ciaran Carson, reprinted by kind permission of the author, The Gallery Press and Wake Forest University Press, N. C. The excerpt from *The Big Sleep* © Raymond Chandler 1939, reprinted by permission of Alfred A. Knopf, Inc. and Hamish Hamilton; the excerpt from *The Killer Department* by Robert Cullen, reprinted by permission of the author and The Orion Publishing Group Ltd; the excerpt from *Murder on Ward Four* by Nick Davies, Chatto & Windus Ltd 1993, reprinted by permission of Rogers, Coleridge & White Ltd; the extract from 'A

INDEX OF
TITLES AND AUTHORS